£4.95

Way Upstream

Ayckbourn

uel French – London

New York – Sydney – Toronto – Hollywood

WAY UPSTREAM

First produced at the Stephen Joseph Theatre in the Round, Scarborough on 2nd October 1981, with the following cast:

Keith	Robin Bowerman
June	Carole Boyd
Alistair	Robin Herford
Emma	Lavinia Bertram
Mrs Hatfield	Susan Uebel
Vince	Graeme Eton
Fleur	Gillian Bevan

Directed by Alan Ayckbourn

Designed by Edward Lipscomb
(A photograph of Edward Lipscomb's set is reproduced on page vi)

Subsequently produced at the National Theatre (Lyttelton) on 4th October 1982 with the following cast:

Keith	Tony Haygarth
June	Susan Fleetwood
Alistair	Jim Norton
Emma	Julie Legrand
Mrs Hatfield	Jane Downs
Vince	James Laurenson
Fleur	Nina Thomas

Directed by Alan Ayckbourn
Designed by Alan Tagg

AUTHOR'S NOTE

This play was originally produced at the Stephen Joseph Theatre, Scarborough, and at the National Theatre using real water, rain and a moving boat. However, as will become apparent, these are not essential.

The play can be produced equally satisfactorily using simulated or imagined water and even a boat with little or no movement. This the author leaves entirely to the discretion and the budget of the director concerned.

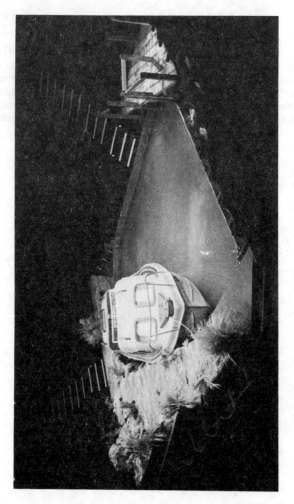

Edward Lipscomb's set for the Stephen Joseph Theatre in the Round

Photograph by Alec Russell

ACT I

A river. The River Orb, in fact. The first evening

We are already considerably inland. Were it, say, the Thames we would probably be in the region of Maidenhead. During the course of the action, we will travel even further upstream some hundred miles where the Orb is far narrower and shallower and becomes finally unnavigable. Thus although at least one bank is always visible (the right-hand one), it should remain fairly unspoilt and indeterminate, providing an adequate but not too man-made a mooring. The aspect, in fact, throughout is definitely rural. The River Orb passes through the most picturesque and deserted of the English countryside. One of the last partially undiscovered rivers

Only one craft is visible, the "Hadforth Bounty". A smallish four-berth cabin cruiser of perhaps 25–30 feet in length, well-appointed, a smart unpretentious little hire craft. Centrally, there is a cockpit open to the skies but with provision apparently for a canvas folding cover to protect it from the rain. This is not, at present, in evidence and is never seen. Forward of this, down two or three steps and through twin doors, a small unseen saloon/galley area and forward of this again, in the very prow, a cramped twin-berth cabin. Both these sections below decks have non-opening portholes. The forward cabin also has a practical opening hatch on to the fore-deck. Aft of the central cockpit another small stairway and similar doors leading first to the toilet cubicle on one side and a similar shower area on the other. Beyond these, the main double cabin. Again, all these below deck aft areas are unseen, except perhaps an occasional glimpse through the odd porthole. The aft double cabin has a roof hatchway opening on to the deck and similar to the one forward

The deck itself is simple and uncluttered. A narrow walkway around the entire perimeter allows braver souls with the aid of an occasional grab rail to work their way from stem to stern. Forward of the cockpit and its windscreen, a raised central area—obviously the roof of the saloon, and intended for sunbathing. Forward of this, a lower part of the deck with the aforementioned forward hatchway, the fixing for the bow rope, at present extended ashore and made fast, and the mud anchor, its own rope neatly coiled beside it. Aft of the cockpit, a similar raised area dropping away to the stern where the aft rope is attached and also made fast. Finally, well to the stern, a small trapdoor to a compartment containing Calor gas cylinders. Below the cockpit floor and accessible by trap doors can be found the inboard diesel engine

It is now well after ten at night on a mild August evening with maybe just a little moonlight. For a moment, silence except for the gentle lap of the water against the boat, the splash of a water creature and the cry of a nightbird. After a second, the sound of voices approaching. Then the beams of torches as people make their way along the towpath towards us

Leading the way is Keith Taylor, a man in his mid to late thirties but clinging a little to the belief that he appears younger. He carries one of the torches and is also laden with cases and belongings. If asked, Keith would probably describe himself as a natural leader — a role he is at present busily fulfilling. Close behind him comes his wife, June, about the same age and also laden. She is attractive and positive and is currently in a filthy temper which she is anxious to let everyone know about

Behind her, Emma, a pleasant, rather nervous, unflamboyant sort of woman, a year or two younger than June. She, too, carries possessions and supplies including one rather large first-aid box to cater for a twelve-day holiday afloat. Finally, bringing up the rear with the second torch, comes Alistair. He is an amiable, vague, rather ineffectual man happy to play second fiddle to Keith or June and even to Emma on occasions. It becomes easy to see how pleasant a man he is to know and how infuriating to live with

Keith ... it must be one of these. Just a tick. (*He shines his torch on the bow of the boat*) Yes, here we are. *Hadforth Bounty*. This is the one.

Emma (*breathless*) Oh, thank goodness. It would be the last one.

Keith (*putting down his burdens*) Wait there, just wait there. (*He clambers into the cockpit*)

Emma (*while he does this*) It looks quite small, doesn't it?

Alistair (*to Keith*) Can you manage?

Keith (*struggling*) Yes, yes. I'm all right.

Emma (*gently*) Shine the torch for him, Alistair.

Alistair I am, I am.

Keith (*safely aboard*) All right, now. Would someone pass me the stuff aboard?

Alistair Oh, yes, I'll ... (*He dithers*)

Keith June. June, my darling. Could you do something, please?

June (*beadily*) What?

Keith Could you pass me your luggage, please? I would like to get your luggage on board if I may.

June begins to do so

Thank you so much. (*As this operation continues*) I will say again, I am very sorry I have kept you all waiting. I'm sorry you had to sit in a pub for two and a half hours, I'm deeply sorry that, as a result of all that, we are starting our holiday four hours late and I am sorrier still that we are having to load this bloody boat in the pitch dark——

June nearly drops something

—careful! — but it was not altogether my fault.

June (*low and fierce*) Keith. There are boats full of people back there trying to sleep.

Alistair (*unhappy at all this*) It wasn't altogether Keith's fault, you know, June.

Emma No, he couldn't help the trains.

June has now handed all her luggage on board including Keith's

Keith Thank you. May I help you aboard?
June I can manage, thank you.
Keith Right, she can manage. Fair enough.

Keith leaves June to struggle aboard whilst he goes to the doorway of the saloon and, in a moment, switches on the forward interior lights

June (*slipping as she boards*) Oh. God.
Alistair (*as the lights come on*) Ah, lights.
Keith All mod cons. (*He moves to switch on the aft cabin lights*)
June (*in great difficulty, grimly*) Aaah! Damn it. Damn it. Damn it.
Emma (*gently as before*) Help her, Alistair, help her.
Alistair Oh yes. (*Starting to put his luggage down*) Do you want any help — er — June?
Keith She doesn't need help. You heard what the lady said.
June Brand new. These were brand new.
Emma (*rather impatiently*) Here, let me, June ...
June I'm all right, I'm all right, I'm all right. (*She hauls herself aboard*)

Keith switches on the cockpit lights

Keith Welcome aboard, darling.
June I told you, Keith, first thing tomorrow morning I'm going straight home.
Keith Fine, fine.

June goes down the saloon steps

Thank you, Emma, I'll take those from you, shall I?

Emma starts to pass her luggage to Keith

June (*from within the saloon*) Oh, dear God, I don't believe it. I don't believe it.
Keith (*taking the large first-aid tin from Emma*) What on earth's this?
Emma First-aid box.
Keith Expecting trouble, are you?
Emma You never know.

From somewhere in the bows an incredulous cry of disgust from June

Keith I mean, I tried to phone. As soon as I saw I was going to be that late, I tried to phone. I tried to phone and say go on without me but, of course, you'd already gone. (*Offering Emma a hand aboard*) Here, Emma.
Emma Thank you.
Keith I mean, I'm not God. Am I? I can't foresee derailments.
June (*from the saloon*) They have just got to be joking. They've got to be joking.
Emma (*picking up one of the life-jackets they have brought aboard*) What are these?
Keith Life-jackets.

Emma Oh. Will we need them?

Keith Good things to have. Good things to have.

June (*emerging from the saloon*) This has simply got to be some joke. If they think anyone's going to sleep in that little broom cupboard ...

Keith Now, come on, darling.

June Have you looked?

Keith We know you're determined to hate everything.

June No, seriously, have you looked?

Keith Yes, you've made your point, don't go on.

June No, please. Take a look. I want you to look.

Keith I don't need to look. I know what's down there. I chose the boat myself. I picked it out and I ordered it.

June You didn't order this boat. You ordered a completely different one.

Keith All right. I ordered a very similar boat.

June You ordered a bigger boat.

Keith You heard the man telling us there was engine failure.

June I heard the man putting you off with some feeble excuse ...

Emma Come on, now, you two, it's very late. (*She starts to pick up some of the luggage in the cockpit*)

June And that is all I heard.

Keith Alistair.

Alistair (*whose thoughts have been elsewhere*) Um?

Keith Would you pass your luggage?

Alistair Oh yes, thanks.

Emma moves towards the saloon

June (*to Emma*) Just go and look in the dog kennel they laughingly call the saloon, Emma. Give yourself a laugh.

Emma Right. (*She goes into the saloon*)

June No, I mean seriously, I mean this has got to be the sickest joke I've ever heard. Four people expected to live on this for twelve days. We couldn't survive. (*She goes down into the aft cabin*)

Keith She's always the same.

Alistair (*handing him a case and smiling*) Happy holidays, eh?

Keith She is always the same.

Emma pops her head up through the forward doorway

Emma It's a sweet little kitchen.

Keith Galley.

Emma Mm?

Keith It's called a galley, love. On boats, they call it a galley.

Emma Oh. Lovely little galley, then. Sweet. (*She disappears again*)

A cry of disgust for June, below

Keith (*helping Alistair aboard*) I mean, I tried to phone. I don't honestly know what else I was supposed to have done.

Alistair Ah, well ...

June emerges from aft

Keith Satisfactory?

June If you like sleeping on a mattress of breeze blocks, terrific.

Keith Splendid. I'm so pleased.

June And the lavatory leaves a great deal to be desired. Is that the only one?

Keith Good Lord, no. There are seven more up forward. Take your pick. What about the shower? Have you seen the shower?

June Yes. I'm dying to rush in and crouch in that. No, seriously, Keith, a joke's a joke but first thing in the morning, I'm sorry, I'm off home.

Emma comes back for more luggage, collects some and goes forward again under the next

Keith Fine. It's your holiday. It's your choice.

June I beg your pardon, this is not my holiday. My holiday when I have one will be in a comfortable hotel, somewhere warm, with a decent bed in a room with space to swing a hamster and not in a floating rabbit hutch on an open sewer. (*She snatches up one small case and goes aft again*)

Keith (*angry*) Terrific. Isn't she terrific? Great woman to be married to. Bags of fun. That's what I've always liked about her. Fantastic sense of adventure.

Alistair OK, Keith.

Keith Of all the women there are in the world. . . .

Alistair It's OK.

Keith Why do we bother, mate, why do we bother?

Emma comes up from forward again

Emma It's a lovely little front bedroom down there.

Keith Forward cabin. That's called your forward cabin.

Emma Yes. Sweet little beds.

Keith Bunks.

Emma Bunks. I think they're just brilliant the way they fit things in in the space. Terribly clever.

Keith Bless you, Emma. Thank you. That is music to my ears. Someone actually enthusing, actually showing some pleasure. So rare, thank you.

Emma Well, you have to make the best of it, don't you? (*Heading aft*) What's down here?

Keith I mean, I don't know what a man has to do, I really don't.

Alistair (*picking up a box of groceries*) I'll take these, er—this way.

Keith Forward.

Alistair Forward.

Keith What are they? Groceries?

Alistair Yes, I think they are . . .

Keith Ah, well. Stow 'em in the galley locker. We can sort things out tomorrow.

Alistair Yes.

Keith We'll try and get an early start tomorrow, shall we? First thing. When the river's at its best. Before the crowds get out.

Alistair Suits me, yes. What about . . .? (*He indicates aft*)

Keith June? Oh, she'll be all right. Means nothing. You know June.

Alistair Ah. Good. (*He goes below with the provisions*)

Keith stands alone for a moment on the deck, his hand on the wheel. He seems content

Emma re-emerges from aft

Emma It's a lovely cabin, that is. Really nice. Quite a lot of room.
Keith Yes, that's the stateroom.
Emma Oh. (*More softly*) She'll be all right, I think.
Keith Yes.
Emma The bed there's not too bad actually. Bunk. A bit lumpy.
Keith You'll be OK in the other ones, will you?
Emma Oh yes.
Keith I mean, we can probably swap round during the week. Once June's settled.
Emma No, it's very cosy in the forward, it really is.

Emma moves back to the saloon nearly colliding with Alistair coming up the steps

Alistair Sorry.
Emma Sorry.
Alistair I put the food box on the floor by the stove.
Emma Yes, I'll sort it out.
Alistair It's fairly late. Don't start too much.
Emma No, I'll just put the milk in the fridge and put the bread away and — then I'm ready for bed. Ready for bunk. (*She goes below*)
Keith She's a nice little craft this, you know, nice little craft.
Alistair Mmm. Mmm.
Keith (*leaning over the side*) Plenty of fenders, you see. That's good, that's good. I mean, the thing about Hadforth boats is, they're not cheap but they'll never rent you rubbish. (*Checking the other side*) There, you see. The same this side.
Alistair Ah, good.
Keith This is going to be a great holiday, Alistair.
Alistair Sure.
Keith No, I mean it, really. It's going to be exciting. It's going to be a challenge. Do you realize this is the first holiday I have had personally for four years.
Alistair Really?
Keith Can you believe that? Four years. And I am going to enjoy it. With or without her.

Emma comes up

I'm saying this is going to be an exciting holiday, Emma.
Emma Oh, yes.
Keith Fresh horizons.
Emma So long as we don't sink.
Keith Sink? You'd have a job to sink this.
Alistair Which way do we go? Up or downstream?

Keith Upstream, of course.

Emma How far are we going?

Keith As far as we can. All the way.

Alistair How far's that?

Keith Armageddon Bridge. That's the limit. You can't navigate beyond that. Not in a craft this size. It's as far as we can go. Be there by next Sunday. That leaves us five days to get back. Downstream, you see. Faster. (*He clambers on to the forward deck*) Look at all this. So peaceful. Isn't this marvellous? When you think that for most of our lives we miss all this, don't we?

Alistair Yes.

Emma Yes.

They all gaze at the water for a second

Well, see you in a minute.

Alistair OK.

Emma (*to Keith*) Good-night.

Keith Good-night, Emma.

Emma goes below. There is the splash of a water-vole

Ssh.

Alistair What?

Keith Ssh. Water-vole. Hear that? Water-vole . . .

Alistair Ah.

Keith (*indicating the aft hatch*) Hatch here, you see. That's handy.

Alistair Did you have a good meeting?

Keith Oh, I think we got it. I think we've got it all right.

Alistair Well. I'm amazed.

Keith I tell you, a small firm like ours, a small factory, low overheads, competitive labour costs, we've got to win hands down. In our own line, we're out on our own. (*Examining the boat*) Beautifully built, this, you know.

Alistair Yes.

Keith Anyway, it's all Martin Cook's problem for the next twelve days. Leave it all to him.

Alistair I hope we can.

Keith Look, I've instructed Martin Cook that he is not to budge one inch from the management line and if he gets any sort of trouble from any employee, whether it be Ray Duffy or any other of his cronies, he's to throw the book at him.

Alistair Ah.

Keith It's time we got tough, Alistair. They're getting no more for nothing. Anything else, they're going to have to work for it. (*Discovering the forward hatch*) Ah, you've got a hatch this end as well. (*Opening it*) It means you can look out at the stars while you're——

Emma (*from within*) Oh, hallo.

Keith (*rapidly closing the hatch*) Oh. Sorry, my love, sorry. (*To Alistair*) Sorry. (*With an embarrassed laugh*) Didn't know they still wore those.

(*Moving back aft*) You know what'll finally bring this country down, Alistair?

Alistair What?

Keith It's when we finally give in once and for all to people like Ray Duffy. When we hand it to him on a plate. Well, I'm sorry. If he wants what's mine, he's going to have to fight me for it.

Alistair I hope it won't come to that.

Keith Don't you? You know, I think I'd rather welcome it.

June comes up from the aft, dressed for bed

June No hot water. Thought you'd like to know.

Keith (*ignoring her*) Anyway, not to worry. I am keeping a sort of eye on things so don't worry.

June Did you hear me? I said there's no hot water.

Keith No, there won't be. We'll need to run the engines for a bit. That operates the heat exchanger.

June Well, isn't this just the jolliest little boat you could imagine? So when can we expect hot water?

Keith About ten o'clock tomorrow morning.

June Then kindly sleep well away from me tonight. (*She goes below*)

Keith Well, I'm not starting the engine now, woman, it's the middle of the night. (*To Alistair*) What does she want me to do? Does she want me to start the engine. Wake everybody up?

Alistair Do you think they're both really going to enjoy this?

Keith June's having a wonderful time. She never felt so hard done by in her life.

Alistair I meant Emma as well. She's—well, she's not really what you'd call the open-air type.

Keith She'll love it. Once we get underway. So much to see.

Alistair She's always happier in towns. I think she finds the countryside rather threatening. She doesn't even go in our garden very much and there's only about nine square feet of that. Prefers the great indoors.

Keith She can stay below then. Keep June company.

Alistair (*dubiously*) Yes. Well, if it's an early start, I'd better ...

Keith Yes, we both should.

Alistair (*moving to the saloon*) Sleep well, then. (*He goes inside*).

Keith And you.

Alistair closes the saloon doors

(*To himself*) Great holiday. It's going to be a great holiday.

Keith gives his surroundings one more approving nod, switches off the cockpit lights and goes below into the aft cabin. He closes the doors behind him.

We are left on the outside of the boat somewhat distant observers. There is a degree of clumping and bumping from both ends of the craft and muffled inaudible conversations. If we could hear them, they would be saying:

June (*muffled*) I haven't bothered to unpack because it isn't worth it.

Keith (*muffled*) Just as you like. Just as you like.

June (*muffled*) I mean you've behaved selfishly in your time but this just about takes the bloody cake. Promising me a holiday for a year and then seriously expecting me to put up with this.
Keith (*muffled*) What's the matter with it?
June (*muffled*) Absolutely unbelievable even from you.

Silence aft. Just clumps and bangs

Alistair (*muffled*) You want this in there?
Emma (*muffled*) Oh, thank you.
Alistair (*muffled*) I'll bring it through.

A loud bump as of someone hitting his head forward

(*Muffled*) Ow!
Emma (*muffled*) That your head?
Alistair (*muffled*) Yes.
Emma (*muffled*) Oh.
June (*muffled*) I mean, what sort of holiday is this going to be for me?
Keith (*muffled*) I haven't the faintest idea.
June (*muffled*) Exactly. Exactly.

More clumps fore and aft. The forward hatch is opened suddenly and Alistair's head pops into view

Alistair ... have this open, shall we?
Emma (*below, unseen*) Do you think we should?
Alistair Why not?
Emma (*below, unseen*) Well, things might get in.
Alistair What things?
Emma (*below, unseen*) Things. Bats and things.
Alistair It's just there's not a lot of air. Look, I'll tell you what. If we turn the light off, we won't attract them.

His head disappears, but the hatch remains open. A second and then, first the saloon and then the forward cabin lights go out. Silence from this end. One or two more clumps aft. Then, the cabin lights go off there too and the craft is in darkness

Time passes. Gentle lapping water. The odd nightbird and animal. The moonlight is now quite bright. Suddenly June's voice is heard

June (*muffled and complaining*) It just never occurred to you, did it, to consider me for a moment? Never even crossed your mind.
Keith (*very loud and quite clear*) June, it's four o'clock in the morning. Now will you please shut up. Just shut up and go to sleep.

The lights in the forward cabin snap on. June's sobs are heard

(*Muffled*) I'm sorry. I'm sorry, baby, I'm sorry.
June (*muffled, weeping*) What's the use? What's the use?

Alistair's head appears through the forward hatchway. He looks puzzled

Keith (*muffled*) I didn't mean that.

June (*muffled*) What's going to happen to us? (*She continues to sob*)

Alistair slams shut the forward hatch. June's crying stops abruptly. The forward cabin lights go out again

(*Muffled*) Can they hear us?
Keith (*muffled*) No.
June (*muffled*) I think they can hear us, you know.
Keith (*muffled*) They can't hear us. Now, shut up, June. Please for the last time, shut up and go to sleep.

Silence, at least from the humans. Dawn comes up on the river. It is the start of a glorious sunny day. Birds and water sounds and the distant chug of other craft getting underway

Keith comes on deck from his cabin. He is now dressed for cruising. Smart white trousers, deck shoes, short sleeve shirt and jaunty captain's cap. He has with him a book — "River Cruising on the Orb" — which is a fairly comprehensive hardback manual and a flipover type map of the route. He sets these down by the wheel and raps on the saloon door

(*Calling*) Come on, then. Come on. All hands on deck.

Alistair emerges with half a bacon sandwich in his hand

Alistair (*slightly inaudibly*) Wha—?
Keith Ready for off?
Alistair (*chewing furiously*) All right, OK. Just a tick. (*He disappears briefly*)
Keith (*shouting through the doorway after him*) Tell the bos'n she better get everything stowed away pretty sharpish.

Keith consults his map. Alistair returns on deck

Now I want to get to Pendon Bridge by twelve noon at the latest. By the end of this afternoon, I think we ought to have reached the lock here at Trill.
Alistair Where?
Keith Trill. (*Showing Alistair the map briefly*) T-R-I-L-L, there, you see.
Alistair Oh, yes.
Keith Right, let's give her a turn. See how she sounds. Come on, my beauty.

He turns the ignition key and starts the engine. After one false start, the diesel engine roars into life

Listen to that, listen to that.

Emma comes out of the saloon

Emma Are we off?
Keith Nearly. (*To Alistair*) Check astern, will you?
Alistair Our what?
Keith Check astern. See that the cooling's working.
Alistair Where?
Keith Go on, have a look.
Alistair (*puzzled*) OK. (*He makes his way astern*)

Keith (*to Emma*) All stowed away?
Emma I think so.
Keith Make sure you are. If we get underway and you're not, you'll be trapped under falling crockery. (*To Alistair*) How's it look?
Alistair Very splendid. What am I looking for?
Keith You see where the smoke's coming out ...
Alistair Yes.
Keith Well, you should be getting water as well. That means your engine cooling system's functioning. Always check that first thing. Otherwise, you're overheating. Eventually, bang. Engine blows up under you.
Emma Oh, God. (*She goes below*)
Keith (*to Alistair*) Stay that end. Stand by to cast off.
Alistair Right.
Keith When I give the word. Wait till I say.

June comes up from the aft cabin

June What's all this ghastly noise?
Keith What do you think it is? It's the engine.
June How long does it go on for?
Keith All the time. Whenever we're moving.
June I'm not living with that.
Keith You're going to have to.
June Not for ten days. Not just for hot water.
Keith I thought you were going home anyway.
June I'm going to have to. (*She starts back below*)
Keith Hang about, we're just going to cast off.
June (*without enthusiasm*) Super. (*She goes*)
Keith Gangplank—all right, here we go.

He springs over the side, unties the bow line, jumps back on board and coils it up and puts it neatly on the foredeck. Alistair, on the stern line, copies Keith

Hold on to that until I give you the word.
Alistair OK. (*He waits on shore*)
Keith (*taking the helm again*) Right, cast off.

Alistair does so and jumps back on board

Don't let your warp trail in the water, will you? Or you'll foul the prop.
Alistair Oh dear, yes, can't have that. (*He coils his rope*)
Keith Coil it neatly.
Alistair Yes.
Keith And away we go.

Keith puts the engine slow ahead. The boat moves forward and away from the bank. Alistair, standing in the stern, looks back. Keith, at the wheel, is in his element

Handles like a dream.
Alistair (*not really hearing him*) Yes?

Keith puts the engines full ahead

Keith This is the life, eh?
Alistair Oh, yes.

They chug along happily. In a while, June comes up on deck. She carries a rug and her beach bag. She wears her skirt and suntop

June You've dressed the part, I see.
Keith You've got to admit it, June, it's terrific. Admit it.

June does not reply. Keith takes this as a moral victory to him and smiles to himself

June (*indicating the deck area over the saloon*) Can I sit up here?
Keith Of course you can. That's what it's for. That's the sun deck.
June Honestly, Keith, it's not the QE2. (*She climbs on to the deck rather cautiously*)
Keith Manage?
June Yes. (*She settles down on the deck*)

Two hoots are heard from a passing craft

Keith (*calling to some craft on the other side of the river*) Morning to you ...
    Yes, isn't it? Gorgeous ... Yes ... (*He smiles and waves. To Alistair*)
    Marvellous thing about the river. Great feeling of camaraderie.
Alistair (*not really hearing him*) Yes.
Keith Only get that on a river.
June What time do you come round with the hot soup?
Keith (*pointing to something on the bank*) Hadforth Brickworks.
June What?
Keith Hadforth Brickworks. Just passing to port.
June Well, wow. I must just dash off a postcard.

A pause as they travel a little further. June lies back and takes no further interest in the journey. Emma comes up from the saloon with two mugs of coffee. She is wearing her life-jacket

Emma Here. Thought you'd like some.
Keith Ah, thank you, my love.
Emma One sugar?
Keith That's it. (*Surveying her*) You don't need to wear that all the time, you know.
Emma I know, I just feel safer with it on.
Keith It's quite safe.
Emma I know. I just feel safer, that's all. June?
June Hallo.
Emma Coffee?
June No, thanks. Not yet. Bit early.
Emma Alistair?
Alistair (*still right at the stern*) Yes.
Emma Coffee? (*She extends the mug*)
Alistair Oh, ta. (*He moves forward*) What have you got on?
Emma My life-jacket.

Alistair You don't need that, do you?

Emma Probably not.

Alistair (*to Keith*) She doesn't need her life-jacket on, does she?

Keith No.

June Has she got her life-jacket on?

Emma Yes.

June Sweet.

Emma (*going back to the saloon rather crossly*) I just feel safer that's all. I don't know why people are making such a fuss.

They travel on a little more

Keith Aha. There's a coot. Do you see it? A coot, there.

Alistair Oh, yes.

Keith Darling.

June (*irritably*) What?

Keith Coot, there, you see. Just gone into the reeds.

June A what?

Keith A coot. Little bird.

June Keith, you don't have to point everything out. It's very boring. This river is bristling with bloody birds.

Keith You can tell it's a coot because of the white flashes on its head and beak. That's how you tell it from the moorhen. It's also slightly larger. (*Pause*) There's another one.

June Oh, dear God. (*She rolls over on her face*)

Alistair You know a lot about rivers.

Keith Just a bit, just a bit.

June He knows nothing. He gets it all out of a book.

Keith And what's wrong with a book? (*To Alistair, brandishing his book*) It's good, this. Very informative. *River Cruising on the Orb.* You ought to read it if you're interested.

Alistair Right.

Keith Mind your heads. Bridge coming up.

It gets darker. Their voices boom

This is the railway bridge.

June Really?

Keith The Pendon-Hadforth loop line. Not used now. Closed under Beeching.

Alistair Ah.

As they emerge into the sunlight, Emma comes up from below again

Emma What was that?

Alistair Bridge.

Emma (*looking behind them*) Oh yes. (*To Keith*) Will I be able to shop somewhere? We need things like milk and bread.

Keith You see along there just coming up?

Emma Yes.

Keith That's Pendon Lock. I'll be stopping there. You can shop in the village.
Emma Oh, super. (*She makes to return to the saloon*)
Keith Going below?
Emma Just for a bit.
Keith Make the helmsman a bacon sandwich, there's a love.
Emma (*a fraction's pause*) Yes, all right.
Keith He's slaving over a hot wheel here.

Emma goes below. In a moment, under the next, a burst of Bach from the saloon as Emma turns on her portable cassette recorder. Alistair moves forward from the stern

(*As he passes*) Everything OK back there?
Alistair Yep.
Keith (*hearing the music*) Ah, music, music. (*Shouting down into the galley*) What's this music? Is it cassette?
Emma (*from below*) Yes. Bach.
Keith Very nautical. Very nice. I've brought some of my James Last collection. We must hear some of those later.
Emma (*from below*) Yes.

June brushes the deck where she is lying, distastefully

June It's filthy dirty up here. Filthy.
Keith (*to Alistair*) Better give these decks a thorough going over this evening.
Alistair Yes.
Keith Before they start to get treacherous.
Alistair Yes. I'll give you a hand if you like.
Keith I see. Thought you might volunteer for that. All left to me then, is it?
Alistair No, I'll do my share.
Keith Fine. Then you do the decks.

Emma comes up from the saloon with a bacon sandwich

Division of labour. I'll take the helm, you do the decks and Emma does the food. Thank you, my angel. Boats are a society in miniature. Everyone has a role, everyone has a function.
Emma What's your function, June?
June Ornament. Sheer ornament.
Emma (*lightly*) I see. Fair distribution of labour, is it?
June It's your toy, dears. You can play with it to your hearts' content. I'm on holiday.
Keith (*appealing to the others*) What can you say to that? I mean, what can you say?
Emma (*struggling on to the fore deck*) Well, I'm going to be an ornament as well, in that case. For a bit.
Alistair (*helping her*) Yes, why don't you get some sun?
Emma No, I just want to sit.
Alistair You could put your new swimsuit on.
Emma (*sotto*) No.

Alistair Why not?

Emma I don't want to.

Alistair I thought you bought it for this.

Emma Yes. I tried it on again last night. I look awful in it.

Alistair You looked very nice.

Emma I didn't. I looked awful. I'm not wearing it. (*To June*) Is there room
for me?

June (*moving a little*) Yes, sure.

Emma It's all right. I just want to sit. I'm not going to lie down. (*She perches
somewhat uncomfortably on the edge of the saloon roof*)

Alistair (*climbing down into the cockpit, to Emma*) Have you washed up?

Emma Not yet.

Alistair I'll do that then.

Emma (*a little surprised*) Oh, thank you.

Alistair goes below into the saloon. The music ends shortly after

Keith (*chuckling*) Division of labour, you see, division of labour.

A horn hoot from another craft. Keith hoots back

Morning. Another nice one, eh? Yes ... yes ... (*He chuckles in reply to
some flattering comment about the two women*) Yes, both mine. Some of us
are just born lucky, eh. (*He munches contentedly on his bacon sandwich in
seventh heaven, being now in control of his craft, and, to a certain extent, his
crew. During the next, he studies his map and his book as he navigates*)

June God, hark at him. He can hardly manage one of us. Heaven help him if
he ever had to cope with two.

*Emma looks behind her to see if Keith has heard. He waves and smiles. Emma
smiles back faintly*

I'm not going to be able to stick ten days of this, you know.

Emma No?

June Do you realize I didn't sleep the entire night. Not at all.

Emma No? Aren't you comfortable?

June (*grimly*) It's hardly the bed, darling, it's hardly the bed. You can't
blame the poor bloody bed.

Emma No?

June Do you know I actually loathe him. Isn't that awful? I utterly loathe
him?

Emma No, you don't loathe him, June.

June (*despairingly*) Oh, Emma, he's just so boorish and unspeakable and
awful. He's an awful man ... Do you know, Emma, there actually are
some men — there really are — who understand women. Intimately. When
they make love to you as a woman, it's as though it were an act of
worship ...

Emma (*rather impatiently*) Oh, God, June ...

June No, really. Honestly. There are men of imagination. Men of finesse,
men of panache, men of ...

Emma *Savoir-faire.*

June Yes. That's it. They're not all insensitive little sex-starved ferrets . . .

Emma giggles, despite herself

No. You mustn't laugh. It's not fair. You've got someone. You're all right. You have someone sensitive and feeling.

Emma How do you know?

June I can tell. It's their eyes, dear. You can always tell from their eyes. Well he is, surely? Sensitive? Isn't he? Alistair?

Emma Oh, yes. Alistair's very sensitive. Terribly.

June It wouldn't be so bad if I could sleep. Do you know I can't sleep at all . . .

Emma Dear . . .

Keith sounds his horn. He's seen someone on the bank ahead

June Why does he keep doing that?

Keith There she is. Hallo there, Mrs Hatfield. Good-morning.

Alistair comes up from below

Alistair Who's that? Is that Mrs Hatfield?

Keith It is indeed. The admirable Vanessa. Good morning, Mrs Hatfield.

Mrs Hatfield appears in the distance. She is a smart woman of about forty, dressed immaculately for the office, but totally unsuitably for a river bank

Mrs Hatfield Yoo-hoo, good-morning.

June What's Mrs Hatfield doing here?

Keith I arranged to meet her.

June You mean, you've lugged the poor woman all the way out here?

Keith I shouldn't think she's complaining. A lovely day. Nice drive to the river. Probably have lunch in a riverside pub. All in the firm's time.

Alistair Yes, but what's she doing here?

Keith I've made arrangements for her to report in.

Alistair How often?

Keith Every day.

Alistair Every day?

Keith If necessary.

Alistair You mean, she's got to come to and fro all the way from——

Keith Look, Alistair, please. You are not the one to give me lectures on how to run things. All right?

Alistair No, but——

Keith Let me just say that while we have people like Martin Cook temporarily in charge of the shop and while we have trouble-makers like Ray Duffy roaming around loose inside it then we have people like Mrs Hatfield reporting back to me on the hour every hour if necessary. OK?

Alistair It's just a hell of a hike for her. That's all I'm saying.

Keith We pay her. She does as she's told. (*He throttles back the engine*)

June Good-morning, Mrs Hatfield. You're looking very summery.

Mrs Hatfield Thank you, Mrs Taylor. Lovely day isn't it? Good-morning, Mr Taylor. Good-morning, Mrs Wingate.

Emma Good-morning, Mrs Hatfield.

Mrs Hatfield Good-morning, Mr Wingate.

Alistair Good-morning, Mrs Hatfield.

Mrs Hatfield I've got a few things in the car for you to sign, Mr Taylor.

Keith All right, Mrs Hatfield, we'll be alongside in a moment. Alistair, could you take the bow line, please.

Alistair Yes, righto. (*He moves towards the stern*)

Keith No, Alistair, the bow line. The one at the front.

Alistair Oh, yes. (*He moves forward*)

Keith Got a few landlubbers on board, I'm afraid, Mrs Hatfield.

Mrs Hatfield Oh, well. Soon find their sealegs, no doubt. (*She laughs brightly*)

Alistair (*passing June*) Excuse me.

June What's going on?

Keith Can you be ready to catch, Mrs Hatfield?

June What are we doing?

Alistair We're docking with Mrs Hatfield.

June I suppose you three are going to have a board meeting or something.

Alistair Probably.

Keith All right, standby, Alistair.

Alistair OK. Just a bit nearer . . .

Keith Alistair, as soon as you've got that line to Mrs Hatfield, can you go aft and be ready to jump ashore with your stern warp. OK?

Alistair (*faintly puzzled*) Yes, I think so.

Mrs Hatfield (*to Emma*) That's lovely, I like that. What is it?

Emma My life-jacket.

Mrs Hatfield Nice colour. Do you have to wear it?

Emma Yes.

Alistair Catch, Mrs Hatfield. (*He throws. The rope falls short*)

June Brilliant.

Alistair Sorry.

Mrs Hatfield Whoops.

Keith It helps if you don't stand on the other end of the rope, Alistair.

Alistair Sorry, coming again.

Alistair throws the rope again, Mrs Hatfield catches it successfully, though it's now very wet

Emma (*encouragingly*) Well done.

Keith OK. Hang on to that, Mrs Hatfield.

Mrs Hatfield I will. Yes. (*She digs her high-heeled shoes into the bank*)

Keith (*warming to his task*) Stand by on the stern line.

Alistair Right. (*He thunders aft past June*)

June This is hell. It's like being in hell.

Mrs Hatfield You're swinging out at the back, did you know?

Keith It's OK. I'll compensate for that. I'll compensate.

Keith revs the engine and turns the wheel hard over. Everyone lurches on deck

Alistair Steady, steady.

Emma Careful, Alistair.
June What are we supposed to be doing?
Keith Sorry.
Mrs Hatfield You're still swinging out.
Keith Well, what are we doing swinging out, we should be swinging in.
Mrs Hatfield I'm sorry, Mr Taylor, you're definitely swinging out.
Keith Well, it's because you're swigging your warp, Mrs Hatfield. Don't swig your warp, keep your warp slack.
June Oh, for God's sake, Keith, will you speak English.
Emma Perhaps if you turn your steering wheel the other way.
Keith Wait a minute, wait a minute.
Alistair We're swinging out in the middle of the river, did you know?
Keith I know, I know. Just a second.

He revs his engine again savagely. Everyone on board lurches again. Mrs Hatfield is dragged several feet

Mrs Hatfield Ah!
June Keith, don't keep doing that.
Emma Oh, heavens.
Keith I have to. I have to. I'm trying to compensate for the torque.
June Well, you're pulling the poor woman in the water.
Keith Oh, God, well then, tie off then. Tie off, Mrs Hatfield. Make fast.
Alistair We're blocking it right across. There's a whole queue of boats behind us.
Keith All right, all right. (*To Emma*) All right, take the helm. Take the helm.
Emma Me?
Keith (*to Emma*) Keep it hard a-port. Hard a-port.
Emma Hard a-port.
Alistair (*preparing to throw the stern rope*) Here she comes.
Keith Alistair, don't throw that, you'll twist it round the prop. (*He rummages for the boat hook*)
Mrs Hatfield I'm sorry, there's nothing to tie this to at all.
Keith Bollard. Use your bollard.
Mrs Hatfield I don't have a bollard.
Keith God, what's the matter with people? (*He makes his way astern with a hook*)
June Keith, you heard her, she hasn't got a bollard.
Keith Alistair, take this. (*He hands him the boat hook*) Give me that. (*He takes the stern line from Alistair*) Now try and push us back towards the bank.
Emma (*frustratedly*) I don't know what I'm doing here. I just don't know what I'm supposed to be doing.
Mrs Hatfield I'm sorry, Mr Taylor, I'm going to have to let go.
Keith No, don't let go. June, in the starboard locker a rond anchor. Throw Mrs Hatfield a rond anchor.
June A what?
Keith Please, June, for the love of mike. Either a rond anchor or a mooring screw. There must be a mooring screw.

June What the hell's a morning screw?
Keith Mooring. A mooring screw.

Hoots from other boats behind them

   (*Shouting back to them*) All right, all right. Just a minute.
Alistair I can't reach the bottom with this.
Keith Emma. Give us a touch astern. Very slow astern, all right? Very gently.
Emma (*tearful*) I don't know what he's talking about. I don't understand what he's saying.
Keith Mrs Hatfield, would you please not keep pulling your warp.
Mrs Hatfield I am not pulling it, Mr Taylor, it is pulling me.

A rev of engine as Emma sends the boat hard astern

Emma Oh, God.
Mrs Hatfield (*losing her rope*) Whoops, there it goes. Sorry.
Keith Emma, what the hell are you doing?
Mrs Hatfield Sorry.
Emma I don't know what I'm doing. I've said, I don't know.
June (*fishing the bow line out of the water*) OK, I've got it.

More hoots

Keith (*roaring at them*) Will you stop that hooting, you stupid bastards? We're doing our best.
Alistair We seem to have lost a bit of the camaraderie of the river.
Keith Now listen, everyone, please. Will you please just listen to instructions and do as you're told. Simply do as I tell you.
June Keith, none of us has a clue what you're talking about. We don't understand all this nautical gibberish.
Keith Dear God. (*He drops the bow line and returns to the cockpit*) I've got a boatload of idiots. Raving, mindless idiots. (*He fishes in the cockpit locker*)
Alistair I think we're moving in actually. It's what you did, Emma.
Emma Oh, was it?
Keith (*producing two mooring irons and a mallet*) Rond anchors. These are called rond anchors, all right?
June Thank you.
Mrs Hatfield Throw me that rope, Mr Wingate and I might be able to reach.
Alistair Right. (*He gives up boat hooking and gathers up the stern line*) A touch more of that engine, Emma, like you did before.
Emma What, like this? (*She revs the engine astern*)

Keith dives for his bow line as it snakes away

Keith What are you doing? Emma, don't do that.
Emma Sorry. Alistair asked me to.
June Total and utter chaos.
Alistair That's better. (*To Mrs Hatfield*) OK.
Mrs Hatfield Right.

Alistair throws the stern line to Mrs Hatfield who catches it

I've got it.

Keith jumps ashore with the bow line and starts to hammer the forward rond anchor into the ground

Emma Well done.
Keith I don't believe it.

June gathers up her stuff from the deck. Alistair perches astern

(*To Emma*) Will you switch off, Emma. Just turn the key.

Emma does so. The engine dies

June Did you say you were going shopping?
Emma We need one or two things.
June I'll come with you. Anything to get off this smelly little tub. (*She goes below to her cabin*)

Emma goes into the saloon. The distant hoot of passing boats. During the next, Keith walks along the bank and hammers in the stern rond anchor

Keith (*smiling and waving in response to the hoots*) Sorry about that. Sorry. (*To Mrs Hatfield*) You've brought some things for signature, have you?
Mrs Hatfield Yes, I'll fetch them, Mr Taylor. They're in the car.
Keith (*taking the rope from Mrs Hatfield*) Mr Cook in control, is he? (*He ties off the stern line*)
Mrs Hatfield Yes, no apparent problems. Mr Duffy has arranged a meeting with him at three o'clock this afternoon. I'm going to try and be back for that.
Keith Oh, Mr Duffy's arranged a meeting, has he?
Mrs Hatfield Yes, he was in first thing this morning.
Keith Thought he might.
Alistair Oh, Lord.
Keith You tell Mr Cook, Mrs Hatfield, that he has my full authority to be as firm with Mr Duffy as he likes.
Mrs Hatfield Yes, Mr Taylor.
Keith He has my full permission to tell Mr Duffy exactly where to put his demands.
Mrs Hatfield Yes, Mr Taylor.
Alistair Keith, I think we ought to first find out if Ray Duffy is representing the general feeling of the workforce.
Keith Mr Duffy represents nobody but Mr Duffy. Am I right, Mrs Hatfield?
Mrs Hatfield I think Mr Cook feels that. He looked very determined——
Keith Good man.
Mrs Hatfield But then, mind you, so did Mr Duffy ...

She goes off to the car

Alistair I still think we should have left someone other than Cook in charge.
Keith Cook's fine. He's got the brains of a neutered parrot but he's all right.

Keith climbs back on board and replaces the mallet. Alistair follows. As they do so, June emerges from her cabin with a jacket on

June Right, we're off shopping. (*Calling*) Emma.
Emma (*from the saloon*) Coming.
Keith Just a sec. Listen, gang, before you go, just a word.

June turns back to her cabin

    June, please.
June Forgot my purse.
Keith Look, this won't take a second. While she's getting the letters. (*Calling*) Emma.

Emma comes up on deck

Emma Yes?
Keith Now listen. I just wanted to say this. I don't want to get heavy but . . . There's a basic rule of the sea . . . and of the river, just as much . . . big ship, small boat like this, doesn't matter.
June Oh, come on, get on with it.
Keith On any boat, there can only be one skipper. OK? One guy who gives the orders. All right? It has to be that way otherwise it's bedlam. Like it was just now. Now, I don't mind taking the job, I don't mind the responsibility but I must have your support. OK? Make sense? OK?
Alistair Yes, fine.
Emma Yes.
June He'll have us all saluting next.
Keith Now, come along, I'm not saying that.
Alistair He's not saying that, June.
Emma No, he's not saying that.
Keith All I'm saying is, there's got to be a bit of order, that's all.
June All right. Ay ay, sir. Fine. Permission to go below? Thank you. (*She goes below*)
Keith What's the point? I mean, what's the point? All I'm saying is there's got to be an element of order. Otherwise, we'll finish up in the weir, that's all I'm saying.
Alistair Yes, that's agreed. You're the skipper.
Keith Emma?
Emma (*guardedly*) If that's what you both want, it's OK by me.
Keith Fair enough then. (*He starts to go down into the saloon*) Alistair, you'd better come. There may be some cheques for you to sign as well. (*He goes below*)
Alistair That's all right, isn't it? Him being skipper? Well, isn't it?
Emma (*short*) Fine. If that's what you want.

Alistair goes down into the saloon a little puzzled

    (*Calling*) June.
June Just a minute. Just powdering my nose.
Emma Ready when you are.

She's about to climb off the boat when Keith reappears from the saloon

Keith (*to Alistair behind him*) I'll need my pen. Oh, Emma.

Emma Yes.

Keith (*with somewhat transparent charm*) You wouldn't be a real angel, would you?

Emma What?

Keith Make us all another cup of coffee before you go. That's a girl. (*He winks at her and goes aft to the cabin*)

Emma (*on the verge of saying something else and checking herself*) Ay ay, sir.

Emma goes below

Time passes. Sunset on the river. The boat is in darkness. Silence except for the usual wild-life noises. This is broken suddenly from aft by a great moan of despair from June, in her cabin

Keith (*muffled, angry*) What the hell do you want from me?

June (*loud, muffled*) I want someone who'll respect me as a woman, that's what I want.

Keith (*muffled*) Oh, Jesus.

The lights in the bow cabin come on

June (*muffled*) That's what I want.

Keith (*muffled*) Sssh.

June (*muffled*) No. Why should I ssh? What have I got to ssh about? I want the whole world to hear this.

Keith (*muffled*) Shut up.

Their voices go down to a murmur. The lights go off in the bow cabin and in a second Alistair comes on deck in his bathrobe. He perches on the saloon roof and lights a cigarette. Emma comes up the saloon steps to join him

Emma Did they wake you again?

Alistair Yes. I don't think I can stand this every night.

Emma Things are apparently a bit awful.

Alistair Yes, I gather.

Emma June was telling me on the way to the village. It's all gone wrong apparently. Poor June. (*Reflecting*) Poor Keith really. (*Reaching for his cigarette*) Give us that a sec.

Alistair I thought you'd given up.

Emma Come on.

Alistair (*handing her the cigarette*) Well, don't throw it in the bilges. It'll blow us up. Skipper wouldn't approve.

Pause

Emma It happened again, didn't it, today?

Alistair What?

Emma Him. Appointing himself skipper. I mean, he just assumed. He never even asked you.

Alistair Me? I wouldn't want to be skipper.

Emma Why not?

Alistair Because I don't know **anything** about **skippering**.

Emma Neither **does** he. He's **just read** that **book, that's all.**

Alistair That's one more book than I've read then, isn't it? Oh, let him be skipper. I don't care. He's having a wonderful time.

Emma Giving us orders.

Alistair Not really.

Emma Why should he? It's not his boat. We've all rented it together. It's our boat. We've all paid our share.

Alistair I think you're getting a bit of a thing about this.

Emma Well, it's the same with the firm. You're supposed to be equal partners. You'd never know it. You and Martin Cook are just sidekicks.

Alistair No, we're not. Well. Only because we want to be. We're good seconds-in-command.

Emma I don't think you are.

Alistair No?

Emma No. I certainly wouldn't have married you if I thought that. I married you because you were a leader.

Alistair Oh? I didn't know that.

Emma coughs

Are you enjoying that?

Emma No.

Alistair Then don't smoke it.

Emma I need it. (*She broods*) Alistair?

Alistair Yep.

Emma (*carefully*) If I was—if you thought I was in great danger, say—ever . . . If I ever needed you because I was in danger and you had to sort of protect me from something or defend me, what would you do? I mean if it was really dangerous for you.

Alistair I'd probably run the other way.

Emma Would you? (*She thinks*) You wouldn't, would you?

Alistair I don't know.

Emma I do hope you wouldn't.

Alistair I don't know what I'd do. I really don't. I'm not much of a hero figure, you know. God, you didn't marry me because you thought I was a hero as well as a leader, did you? This is all too much. Anyway, I thought it was all a bit old hat. I didn't think women went in for that any more. Charging white knights and all that.

Emma It's nice to dream about though, sometimes.

Alistair Well, don't dream about me will you? I'm frightened of horses as well.

Emma Oh, Alistair.

Pause

Armageddon Bridge. Very romantic, isn't it?

Keith (*muffled*) Come on, then, you tell me. You tell me.

June (*muffled*) Ssh.

Keith (*muffled*) You know so bloody much about what's normal and what's average.

June (*muffled*) Will you keep your voice down?

They tail away to a murmur again

Emma It would have probably been better on our own, wouldn't it? On reflection.

Alistair Yes, I did have that idea originally. Just us two. You and me.

Emma Why didn't you suggest it? I thought you wanted to go with Keith.

Alistair Well, I thought you'd get a bit bored with just me after two weeks. And you and June seemed to get along. And so ...

Emma We're not that friendly. Not really.

Alistair Well, I'm not all that potty about Keith, actually. I mean, he's all right but ...

Emma It would have been nice just us.

Alistair I should have suggested it, shouldn't I? (*He smiles*) You know I had this idea, this day-dream, we'd just cruise up the river until we got to this island somewhere – a very small island. Deserted. And then – I don't know ... Well ...

Emma What?

Alistair Well, we'd – I'd – er – we'd swim. Off the boat and we'd get on this island. And.

Emma And what?

Alistair We'd sort of sit there for a bit.

Emma Oh.

Alistair Well ...

Emma (*a bit disappointed*) Is that all?

Alistair Yep.

Emma I'm a rotten swimmer, you know that.

Alistair Yes.

Pause

I think they're asleep now. Shall we risk going to bed?

Emma Do you still love me, Alistair?

Alistair Yes.

Emma Do you still want me? Physically, I mean?

Alistair (*embarrassed*) Er – yes. Yes. Sure ...

Emma (*suddenly equally embarrassed*) Sorry, I shouldn't – sorry ...

Alistair That's all right. No, I mean. Yes. Bit difficult now on the boat but ...

Emma It's all right, you don't have to ...

Alistair I mean, if I haven't it's only because ...

Emma No, no, I'm not ...

Alistair It's not – it's not – it's not you. I promise.

Emma No, I didn't mean that ...

Alistair Good. Because it isn't ...

Emma I know ...

Alistair Really.

Emma Don't worry.

Alistair No.

Emma Don't worry for me.

Alistair No.

Pause

Emma Time for bed.

Alistair Yes. Better get some sleep. Brush up on my heroic powers of leadership. (*He goes down into the saloon*)

Emma (*following him*) I didn't mean that either. (*She goes below*)

Pause. Dawn comes up on the river. Another fine day. Keith comes bounding on to the deck dressed similarly to yesterday including, of course, his skipper's hat. He is whistling a jaunty nautical air

Keith All right, all right. All hands on deck, show a leg there. (*He bangs on the doorway of the saloon*)

Alistair (*appearing, munching*) Just a minute. Still having breakfast.

Keith Breakfast at ten past nine. I had mine at seven.

Alistair Yes. We heard you. What's the hurry?

Keith I want to get through Trill Lock before it gets crowded and as far as Gessing Lock by midday. (*Calling down*) Come on, Emma, stand by to cast off.

Emma comes on deck struggling into her life-jacket

Emma I'm coming, I'm coming.

Keith You take the bow line, Alistair take the stern.

Emma Yes. That's the one, isn't it? Fine.

Emma goes ashore forward and starts to unfasten the bow line. Alistair goes aft and unfastens the other. Meanwhile, Keith starts the engine with a roar

Keith (*calling over the din*) Don't forget the rond anchors.

Alistair OK. OK.

Emma pulls the bow rond anchor out of the ground. Alistair on the stern line has more difficulty. Keith watches him, amused. June comes up on deck. She glares at Keith but does not speak to him

Mrs Hatfield appears in the distance, waving

Mrs Hatfield (*distant*) Yoo-hoo ...

June That's not Mrs Hatfield again?

Emma Looks like her.

June If I didn't know Keith better, I'd say they were having a thing ... (*She takes up her sunbathing position*)

Keith She's met us early for some reason ...

Mrs Hatfield Yoo-hoo. Morning.

Keith Good-morning, Mrs Hatfield.

Mrs Hatfield Good-morning, Mr Taylor. So sorry to rendezvous so early. Good-morning, Mrs Taylor. Good-morning, Mrs Wingate.

Emma Good-morning, Mrs Hatfield.

June Hallo.

Alistair Good-morning, Mrs Hatfield.

Mrs Hatfield Good-morning, Mr Wingate.

Keith Coming aboard? (*He switches off the engine*)

Mrs Hatfield Well, Mr Taylor, I feel you may wish to come ashore.

Keith Come ashore?

Mrs Hatfield To talk with Mr Cook personally by phone.

Keith Why? What the hell's going on, then?

Mrs Hatfield Well, his meeting yesterday with Mr Duffy was rather acrimonious, I'm afraid. Basically because Mr Cook failed to accept that Mr Duffy was speaking on behalf of many other people besides himself.

Keith Was he indeed?

Mrs Hatfield I think a fair number.

Keith I see. Now he's beginning to stir it up. Usual pattern isn't it? Little insects. They come out of your woodwork. Wait there, I'll get my jacket ... (*He marches towards the aft cabin*)

June (*without shifting in her sunbathing position*) Now, don't go mad, Keith. Don't go mad will you ...

Keith I'm stopping this. Once and for all. (*He goes below to his cabin*)

Mrs Hatfield (*to Alistair and Emma*) I think it's still possible to find a solution, even now. But people are getting very entrenched ...

Emma Perhaps one of you ought to go back. Rather than just phoning.

Mrs Hatfield Well yes, that would be ideal, of course. Not that one wants anyone to interrupt their holiday but ... It is serious.

Emma Alistair.

Alistair Mmm?

Emma Do you think you ought to go back? Try and sort this out?

Alistair Oh, no. Not me. Keith. Keith should be the one to go.

Emma Why not you?

Alistair I'd be no use.

Mrs Hatfield Well, in actual fact, Mr Wingate, I think you're underestimating yourself. You see, I think possibly you'd be — well, one hesitates to say better than Mr Taylor — of course, one's not saying that — but you are perhaps in this instance, a fraction more objective. I'm sure you'd have the trust of both parties.

Emma There, you see.

Alistair No — it's really — really not my area. Keith's the man.

Keith comes up from his cabin. He's brushed his hair and put on his blazer

Keith All right. Let's find a phone.

Mrs Hatfield There's one just as you're coming into the village ... (*She moves off*)

Emma We were just wondering if Alistair ought to go back——

Keith Go back?

Emma See if he can calm things down.

Keith You want to go back?

Alistair No — not really——

Keith Go back if you want to——

Alistair No.

Keith Don't think it'll do you any good.

Emma Mrs Hatfield was saying it's possible Alistair might——

Alistair Look Keith, I might as well run her up to the lock for you. Save you coming back. You could meet us there.

Keith Really?

Alistair Why not——

Keith Can you manage that?

Alistair I should think so. I won't try going through the lock. Don't worry.

Keith (*torn between going on after Mrs Hatfield and stopping to argue*) Right.
Well, go carefully.

Alistair Yes.

Keith Keep her speed low.

Alistair Naturally ...

Keith (*as he goes*) Keep over to starboard. Right of the river.

Alistair Will do.

Keith (*in the distance*) Keep away from the weir ... Make sure you know
which is the Lock Cut.

Alistair Sure.

Keith goes off after Mrs Hatfield. They both exit

*A short pause. Emma looks at Alistair. Alistair looks at Emma. June dozes on
in the sun*

Emma Well. You're on your own now, matey. I don't know anything about
it ...

Alistair Yes, OK. I'll — start the engine.

Emma I'll do the ropes.

Alistair starts the engine

Alistair So far so good.

Emma (*loosening the bow line*) Which one shall I let go of first?

Alistair Don't think it matters. That one.

Emma Right.

She throws the rope on board. It lands, perhaps deliberately, on June

June Hell.

Emma Sorry.

June Careful.

Emma (*loosening the stern rope*) OK?

Alistair Go ahead. Give it a push off as you climb on, will you?

Emma Right. (*She clambers aboard the stern getting more agile each time she
does it, and starts coiling up the rope*)

Alistair (*meanwhile*) All right. Here we go. (*He puts the engine into gear*)

A grating sound from under the boat

Emma What's happening?

Alistair Don't know.

June What on earth are you doing?

Emma I think we're going backwards.

Alistair Are we?

Emma It says on the thing. What's it say on the thing?

Alistair Er ... (*Crouching to look*) Astern.

Emma Yes, that's backwards. Ahead. You want ahead.

Alistair Yep. I've got it.

Alistair sends the boat ahead. The grating ceases

Emma That's better.
Alistair Do you think I've damaged it?
Emma I shouldn't think so. We'll soon know, I suppose.
Alistair How?
Emma It'll probably start sinking.
Alistair Oh.
Emma (*joining him in the cockpit*) Well done, anyway. We're underway.
Alistair Yes.
Emma Is it easy?
Alistair Oh yes. You turn the wheel that way, you see, and it goes that way.
   On the other hand, if you turn the wheel this way, it goes this way.
Emma Complicated.
Alistair Oh, terribly.
Emma Here's his book here, you see. It's got everything. (*Flipping through*)
   Bridges — locks — a whole chapter on locks ... signals — buoys. Wildlife.
June There's a boat coming.
Alistair Yes. I see it.
Emma Big one.
Alistair Yes. Pleasure boat I think. So long as it keeps to his side.

Ahead, in the distance, two deep loud hoots from the pleasure craft

Emma What does that mean?
Alistair I don't know. Just hallo, I think.
Emma Hoot back.
Alistair Should I?
Emma Keith always does.
Alistair OK. Let's give them a couple of ... (*Locating the hooter*) Here we
   are. (*He gives two hoots*)

In the distance, two more short hoots from the steamer

   (*Laughing*) Getting quite a conversation going. (*He gives two more single
   short hoots*)
Emma Why is he turning this way?
Alistair Mm?
Emma He seems to be steering towards us now.
Alistair Does he? (*Pause*) My God, he is.
June That thing's heading straight for us.
Alistair Yes, OK June, OK.
Emma He must have seen us.
Alistair Of course he's seen us. Mad idiot. (*He gives three short hoots*)
Emma (*shouting out*) Get out of the way.

Two short blasts from the steamer again, closer this time

   I wonder if all these hoots mean something. (*She starts to examine the
   book*)

June He's getting very close, you know.

Alistair I know. I can see, June, I can see. (*He hoots again. A single hoot*) What does he think he's doing?

Emma (*finding her place in the book*) Hey now, listen to this. Listen. (*Reading*) "One short hoot—I am going to starboard. Brackets to the right. Two short hoots—I am going to port. Brackets to the left. Three short hoots—I am going astern." You've just given three short hoots, haven't you?

Alistair Probably.

Emma That means you're going backwards.

Alistair I'm not going backwards.

Emma I know you're not but you've just told him you were.

Two more short hoots from the steamer, very loud and very close

Now, two short hoots, that means——

June (*panicking*) It means get out of his bloody way.

Emma Wait, give him four short hoots.

Alistair Four?

Emma That's the safest. It means I am not able to manoeuvre.

Alistair About sums it up really. (*He gives four short hoots*)

Emma That's it.

Alistair gives another one by mistake

Alistair Whoops, sorry. Didn't mean that one. (*Shouting to the steamer*) I didn't mean that one.

Emma You shouldn't have done that. Four short hoots followed by another single short hoot means I am turning completely around to starboard. Whereas four short hoots followed immediately by two short hoots means——

June (*screaming*) LOOK OUT!

An enormous long deafening hoot as a very big craft passes them very close. They go into shadow. The boat lurches with the wash. June is rolled practically off the deck with a scream. Alistair and Emma are hurled across the cockpit. A crash and clatter of items falling down in the saloon. A stunned silence. The boat's engine has stalled

Alistair All right?

Emma Yes, I think so.

Alistair That was—er—that was——

Emma That was terrifying. I don't know how he missed us.

June Alistair.

Alistair All right, June?

June We were nearly killed, do you realize that, Alistair? You nearly killed us all, you idiot.

Emma (*going into the saloon*) It wasn't all his fault.

June What do you mean, it wasn't his fault?

Alistair Confusion of signals.

June (*packing up her stuff*) I'm not sitting up here, anymore. You're a
  maniac. (*She starts climbing down into the cockpit*)
Alistair Should be all right now.
June I'm going to find my life-jacket.

*June goes below aft. Emma comes up from the saloon. Alistair restarts the
engine*

Emma There's one or two things broken but we can replace those.
Alistair Oh, dear. Skipper's not going to be too pleased. (*He puts the engine
  into gear*)

*A grinding sound from under the hull of the boat and the threshing of a
protesting engine. A squawk from June in the aft cabin*

  Hell.
Emma We've run aground, haven't we?
Alistair Feels like it.
Emma Oh dear. Can you reverse it?
Alistair I'll try. (*A vain whirring sound*)

June comes out of her cabin

June What are you doing now? I've just spilt half a bottle of handcream.

Ignoring her, Emma takes up the boat hook and goes to the stern

Alistair Any good?
Emma Try again.

Alistair tries again. The engine whirrs to no effect

June Look, what's going on?
Emma Wait a minute, I'll come up front.

Alistair tries reversing again

June Alistair, will you please tell me what you're doing?
Alistair Er—we're just a bit stuck.
June Stuck?
Emma (*in the bows, trying to get some purchase with the boat hook*) Try again
  now.

Alistair does so. No effect

June Do you mean you've run us aground?
Emma And again.

Alistair does so

  No.
Alistair Oh. (*He shrugs and switches off the engine*)
June My God, he's run us aground.
Emma It's hopeless. I think we're really stuck.
June This man has actually run us aground.
Emma Oh, do shut up, June.

June It is unbelievable. In the space of two minutes, we've been practically mown down and now we're shipwrecked.

Emma We're not shipwrecked. We're just stuck on some mud, that's all. Keith's going to laugh his head off, isn't he?

June I'm not stopping on here with you two. I'm off. I'm leaving.

Emma You can try. You'll get very wet and muddy.

June (*running from one side of the craft to the other*) Oh, this is wonderful, isn't it? We're marooned as well. What are we going to do? What are we going to do?

Alistair Look, I'll tell you what. I'll climb over the side and——

June Help. Help. Somebody help us, please.

Alistair I'll climb over the side and I'll try pushing us off. If you could ease us backwards as I push.

June Help. Help.

Emma June, will you please shut up.

June I'm trying to attract someone's attention.

Emma Well, there's nobody here, is there? We're in the middle of a marsh. Now, there's no reason why we can't get off here providing we don't panic. We've just——

Vince's voice is heard, off

Vince (*off; distant*) Hallo. Ahoy. Hallo.

June What's that?

Alistair Someone over there.

Vince appears on the bank

Vince Hallo.

He is a well-built man in his late thirties or early forties, sunburnt and attractive. He wears cut-off denim shorts, a worn denim shirt open to the waist. Around his neck a gold chain attached to a pendant or talisman. A knife hangs from his belt. June unashamedly goggles at him

Hi. Need any help?

June Oh, thank you. Thank you very, very much. We most certainly do.

Vince Got the wrong side of the marker, have you?

Alistair 'Fraid so.

Vince Easy thing to do. Happens to the best of them. Wait a moment. (*He removes his slip-ons*) Can I throw you these?

Alistair Yes.

Vince Heads. (*He tosses his shoes into the cockpit*) Right now. (*He slides down the bank into the water and wades towards the bows*)

June Careful.

Vince It's quite safe. It's not deep.

June Oh, thank goodness.

Vince That's why you ran aground. Start your engine if you would.

Alistair Righto. (*He does so*)

Vince OK now, slow astern.

Alistair (*doing so*) That all right?

Vince (*leaning his shoulder against the prow*) Gently now. Touch more. Touch more. That's it. That's it.

June What an amazing man. Look, he's pushing the boat. He's pushing the boat.

Vince She's coming. She's coming. Ease off. Ease off.

Alistair throttles back

There she floats.

Emma Well done.

June Bravo.

Vince (*heaving himself aboard*) Just a little push, that's all it needed.

Alistair We're really very grateful.

Vince Are you the skipper?

Alistair Er — no, I'm just the temporary skipper. The real skipper's up at the lock. Up at Gessing Lock.

Vince Is that where you're heading?

June That's right.

Vince Going upstream, eh?

Emma That's the idea.

Vince Vince Grant, how do you do.

Alistair Oh, I'm Alistair Wingate. My wife, Emma. And June Taylor who is married to the skipper.

June How do you do. Your shoes.

Vince Thanks. (*Sitting on the edge of the cockpit and putting them on*) Would you mind if I suggested something?

Alistair What?

Vince May I take her up to the lock for you?

Alistair Oh, well ...

June Yes, do. Please do.

Vince I just happen to know this stretch very well. It's a little treacherous.

Alistair No, go ahead.

June Lovely. Our own pilot.

Vince Nice craft.

Alistair Yes.

Vince Handle quite well, don't they?

Alistair Oh, yes.

Vince revs the engine astern and manoeuvres with some confidence

June (*watching him admiringly*) You're used to boats, I take it.

Vince Born on them, born on them.

June Really?

Vince (*moving the craft forward*) Now then, Gessing Lock next stop, eh?

June (*laughing*) Well, thank goodness we're in safe hands at last.

Emma (*rather sourly*) I'll just go and tidy up in the galley.

Vince Oh? You the cookie, are you?

Emma Er — yes. On occasions, yes.

Vince Most important person on board, the cookie. Isn't that true, Skipper?

Alistair Yes, oh yes.

Emma goes below to the saloon

Vince Come far?
Alistair Just from Hadforth. Our second day.
June I'm afraid we're all totally new to this.
Vince All at sea, eh? (*He laughs*)

June laughs

Ah well, once you get the boat bug—Virus Nauticus—that's it.
June Yes, yes, I can see it could be. Yes.
Alistair Are you on holiday?
Vince Permanently. What I always say is life is a holiday.
June How true, how true.
Vince Life is a holiday from death.
Alistair Ah.
June What do you do, Mr Grant? For a living.
Vince Vince. Well, at the moment I rescue attractive damsels in distress.
June Do you have a boat of your own?
Vince Not any more. I used to have a forty-two foot convertible flying bridge twin-screw. Coastal cruising mostly. Did a few good hundred miles in her, I can tell you. The Med., all over.
Alistair What happened to her?
Vince Pirates got her.
June Pirates?
Vince Financial pirates. I couldn't keep up the payments.
June Ah.
Vince No, I'm afraid I'm what you might describe, at the moment, as a victim of the system.
Alistair Oh dear.
June How sad.
Vince You in business, are you?
June Yes, my husband and Mr Wingate are in partnership. We have a small factory. Novelty goods.
Vince Novelty goods.
June Souvenirs, that sort of thing.
Vince (*to Alistair*) You're a managing director, then?
June Well, really we're all directors. I'm a director, Mrs Wingate—Emma's a director.
Vince This is a very high-powered crew, then.
June Oh yes, nothing but the best.

Alistair wanders away towards the stern, slightly embarrassed by June's over-affability

Vince (*pointing*) Water-vole, see.
June (*intrigued*) Oh, yes. Sweet.
Vince I used to have two great danes. Solomon and Sheba. Lived on the boat. Beautiful dogs. They had to go as well.
June Tragic.

Vince You always been a managing director, then?

June Oh no. That's quite recent. Actually, I was in show business before that.

Vince Were you now, were you? Dancer?

June A singer principally.

Vince (*doubly impressed*) A singer. Well.

June We were a group actually. Very young at the time, and we got our first professional engagement in Torquay, would you believe?

Vince I know it well. I know it well.

June That's where I met my husband, actually.

Vince Was he in the group?

June Oh no. He was attached to the entertainments department. I think he was responsible for booking us.

Vince What were you called, the group?

June Oh golly. Gosh. I blush to say.

Vince Go on, what were you called?

June Well, we called ourselves The Gingernuts.

Vince The Gingernuts.

June Stupid. We all had red hair. At that time.

Vince The Gingernuts.

June We only did the one season. I don't think we were frightfully good.

Vince (*disbelievingly*) Ah.

June Anyway, soon after that I married my husband and that was the end of my show business career.

Vince Great story. It's a wonderful world. Show business. There she is. Gessing Lock. And could that be your husband?

June Yes, yes, that's him.

Vince I can spot a managing director anywhere.

Alistair (*moving back to the cockpit*) Is that the lock coming up?

Vince Yes. If you pass me the line from the sharp end, I'll deal with it. You take the back one, OK?

Alistair Yes, right.

Emma (*coming up from below*) Are we there? Want a hand?

Vince It's OK, Cookie, we can handle it.

Emma (*disappointed*) Oh. Right then.

Vince Don't want to risk the cookie, do we? (*He throttles back the engine*)

Keith appears on the bank

June Hallo.

Keith (*puzzled*) Hallo. Whose—?

June We've got a new member of the crew.

Keith So I see. Who—?

June A white knight who rescued us when we ran aground.

Keith Ran aground?

Vince It's OK, Skipper, nothing serious. Nothing to worry about.

Keith How the hell did you run aground?

Emma A slight misunderstanding of river etiquette.

Vince Don't clap them in irons, Skipper, it could have happened to anyone. There you go.

Vince stops the engine and switches off all in one. Then leaps ashore with the bow rope which he ties off briskly. Alistair does the same with the stern line. When he's done this and under the next, he locates the mop and bucket, takes some water from the river and starts to swab the deck

June This man's been simply wonderful.

Vince Not at all.

Keith Well, thank you very much, Mr—er ...

Vince Vince. Vince Grant. Pleased to know you, Skipper.

Keith Keith. Taylor. You've met everyone else?

Vince Oh yes.

Keith Trust them to run it aground, eh? (*He laughs*)

Vince (*laughing*) Yes.

Pause

Well. If I can be of no further service, I'll be on my way.

June Are you off? Where are you off to?

Vince Oh, nowhere special. Keep wandering on upstream a little way.

Keith On foot, are you?

Vince Oh, yes. That's the only way to see the river. Well, I won't keep you. Thanks for the ride, good to have met you.

Despite his goodbye, Vince shows no sign of moving away. Rather, he sits on the bank a little way from them, takes off his shoes, empties them and brushes the soles of his feet. Keith sidles up to him.

Keith (*rather embarrassedly*) Er—would you care for a drink?

Vince A drink?

Keith (*producing a note from his pocket*) With us. Would you like to buy yourself a drink? On me. Here.

Vince Oh no, Skipper. No. Please. I never accept payment. Not for good turns.

Keith Ah. Well, I'm sorry. I didn't—er ... Fine.

Vince Little rule of mine. If it's all the same to you.

Keith climbs back aboard

June Isn't that typical? Typical of Keith. He tips everyone. Quite indiscriminately.

Emma (*sotto, to Keith*) I don't think he's the sort of man you tip.

Keith There's no such person as a man you don't tip.

Emma You wouldn't accept a tip, would you?

Keith Yes, I would.

June Only they call it an inducement.

Keith All right? We'd better get underway.

June I think if we're going to thank him, we should do it properly. We should ask him back on board and offer him a drink. Not try slipping him dirty pound notes like that. So insulting.

Keith We don't want to ask him on board.

June He's saved our lives. We can at least give him a drink.

Emma We've nothing to drink.

June We've my bottle of wine I bought yesterday.
Emma Oh yes.
Keith We don't know who he is.
June He is a thoughtful, kind human being who went out of his way to help us.
Keith Well, I don't want him aboard. I don't know him.

Vince, who has apparently heard none of this muttered conversation, now gets up and moves off

Vince See you then.
Emma Bye.
Keith Goodbye.
Vince *Bon voyage.*
Alistair (*still mopping the deck*) Cheerio. Thanks again.
June I say——
Vince Hallo?
June We were just on the point of opening a bottle of wine. Would you care for a glass with us?
Vince (*turning*) Ah.
June We usually have a glass around this time ...
Keith (*muttering*) Oh, my God.
June Would you care to join us?
Vince Well, I'll say this. Pushing boats single-handed is thirsty work. I won't say no.
June Super. Come aboard.
Emma (*going down into the saloon*) I don't even know how many glasses we've got.
June Alistair, we're all having a glass of wine. Come on.
Alistair OK.
Vince This is very kind. After you, Skipper.
Keith Thank you. (*He starts down the saloon steps*)
June (*gushing*) I don't know what it's like, we bought it in the last village. It'd probably been in their window for three years.
Vince As long as it's wet.
June It's certainly that.

June and Vince go into the saloon. Alistair continues his mopping. Social voices from the saloon, especially June's and Vince's. A cork pops. Emma comes back on deck

Emma Are you coming down?
Alistair (*unhappily*) Yes.
Emma (*not too unkindly*) Oh, Alistair. You are hopeless sometimes, aren't you? Really hopeless.
Alistair Yes, I know. Sorry.
Emma Oh dear.

She goes back down into the saloon. Alistair follows her slowly, leaving his mop and bucket in the cockpit

Time passes once more on the river. The chatter and laughter in the saloon continues. It grows darker, the lights go on in the saloon. Finally, the party breaks up. Vince is the first to come on deck. Everyone, including him, has had a certain amount to drink

Vince ... No, no, enough's enough. I've imposed on you enough.

June (*following him*) Rubbish.

Vince I only came aboard for a drink. I've had a couple of bottles and two meals.

June And you've utterly deserved it. Hasn't he, Keith?

Keith (*coming on deck*) Absolutely. The least we can do.

Vince (*overwhelmed by their generosity*) Well, I don't know what to say ...

Emma (*emerging momentarily*) I'm making up the bed in the saloon for you.

Keith There you are, there you are, you see.

Vince Well, thank you, Cookie, God bless you. I'm used to sleeping rough, I don't need much.

June You've torn us off rocks barehanded, you've steered us through dozens of locks ...

Keith Three. Three locks.

June All right, three locks. You've captained us magnificently.

Keith No, he's not the captain.

Vince No, he's the captain. I'm the pilot.

Keith Get it right. He's the pilot.

June Well, whatever.

Keith Only one skipper, eh?

Vince Definitely. You're the skipper.

June Well, anyone but Alistair. He really is a useless man, isn't he? One glass of wine this evening, he collapses. Poor Emma ...

Keith Ssh. Now——

Vince Can't beat the river on a night like this. Wouldn't want to be anywhere else in the world. Nowhere.

June And you've been around by the sound of it.

Vince Well, courtesy of Her Majesty's government.

Keith Commandos, you say.

Vince Yes.

June Well, we'll sleep safe in our beds tonight.

Vince I hope you do.

June Good-night, then. See you in the morning.

Vince Thank you for your food, your wine and your charming company.

June (*coyly*) Oh, 'twas nothing, sir.

Vince Good-night—Gingernut.

June trills with laughter and goes below

Keith She told you about that, did she?

Vince Were they really called that?

Keith The Gingernuts. Four redheads, a smile and a song. They were dreadful. People were fighting to get out. Lost me my job, actually. I was responsible for booking them.

Vince Ah.

Keith Er — you didn't take it amiss what I was saying about being skipper?

Vince Not at all.

Keith I mean, it has to be said. There's only one skipper.

Vince Dead right.

Keith You have to make that clear. Let people know who's the boss.

Vince True.

Keith It's sometimes a hard thing to say but then it takes a hard man to say it. You know what I mean?

Vince I do.

Keith I'm the skipper. This is my boat.

Vince Sure.

Keith That's my wife. OK? You know what I'm saying, Mr Commando? My wife.

Vince Certainly.

Keith And there's nothing there for you. All right?

Vince I never imagined there was, Skipper.

Keith Good. So. OK. No offence?

Vince None taken, Skipper.

Keith Only one false step and I'll throw the book at you. Good-night.

Vince Good-night to you, Skipper.

Keith goes down into the aft cabin and closes the doors

Vince is left standing on the deck alone. He starts to whistle to himself very softly. He moves and stands by the wheel for a second. He picks up Keith's "River Cruising on the Orb" and looks through it, cursorily, still whistling quietly. He snaps the book shut and casually, with a flick of the wrist, flips it over the side and into the water. As Vince goes quietly down the stairway and into the saloon closing the doors behind him, the Lights fade to a Black-out

CURTAIN

ACT II

The same. It is another glorious morning on the fourth day of the cruise. One day later in fact. We are further upstream than we were by fifteen to twenty miles, near Stumble Lock

Vince comes on deck from the saloon. He surveys the river, breathing deeply for a second. After a moment, he springs into action, bounding on to the aft deck and then working his way forward as he starts to awaken the boat's other occupants, slapping on the decks with the palms of his hands

Vince Come on, then, let's be having you. Let's be having you. Good-morning. Good-morning. Time to get up. Rise and shine. Come along there.

Several groans from within. As Vince reaches the bows, Keith comes out of the aft cabin still in his pyjamas

Keith What is it? What's the matter?

Vince Good-morning, Skipper. Sorry, did I startle you?

Keith My God, what's the time?

Vince Seven-thirty. You wanted to be on the move early. I thought I'd wake you.

Keith Yes, thank you.

Vince You have to be somewhere by noon again, haven't you?

Keith Yes, I've arranged to meet Mrs Hatfield at Slippey Lock ... (*Still trying to focus his eyes*) Sorry, I'm a bit ...

Vince Oh dear. Yes, I could hear you had a bit of a rough night.

Keith Really, what did you ...?

Vince Nothing. I heard nothing. Only that you were having a rough night. You don't mind me hitching another ride today, Skipper?

Keith Good Lord, no—

Vince Well, it's been two nights now. You just say the word.

Keith No. I can do with you around, Vince.

Vince Well, I realize you're saddled with a slightly tyro crew.

Keith True. True. Well, I'll get——(*He makes to move aft*)

Vince Skipper.

Keith Yes.

Vince It just occurred to me, Skipper, I don't know how you'll react to this — it might help if we tried switching the duties round a bit. Gave everyone a share of the responsibility.

Keith How do you mean?

Vince You know, someone at the helm one day, someone in the galley the next. Get more of a team feeling. So everyone feels they're doing their share.

Keith Yes, yes. Good point. I'm not altogether sure about Alistair going back on the helm but . . .

Vince (*smiling*) Well, maybe we could rig the roster a little. But Emma or June, they could have a go.

Keith Emma, yes.

Vince We could try Alistair in the gallery. Put him on the cooking.

Keith (*dubiously*) Yes. Yes.

Vince Well, let's face it. He's going to be a liability wherever you put him. He's not a river man, is he?

Keith No, he's not a river man. So Emma at the helm, Alistair in the galley. What about June? Always assuming she'll join in.

Vince We could start her on cabin maintenance, make sure everything's shipshape below. Clearing up generally.

Keith I don't think she'd—er . . .

Vince I think if she sees we're all mucking in, Skipper . . .

Keith Maybe. Er, right, what shall I do?

Vince Of course. Now, what's left? Deck maintenance.

Keith Deck maintenance?

Vince Make with the old mop and bucket. Show them the skipper can muck in.

Keith Yes. Right. Just for today, this is?

Vince Oh yes, tomorrow we'll all move round.

Emma comes on deck from the saloon

Emma Good-morning.

Vince Good-morning, Cookie.

Keith Er—we've decided you're going to take the helm today, Emma.

Emma What?

Vince You're in the driving seat.

Emma Me?

Keith Everyone's going to take turns. Your turn today.

Emma Oh no . . .

Vince Nothing to it.

Keith Vince'll show you.

Vince I'll show you.

Emma Well, if nobody else wants to. You want me to take it through locks and things?

Vince Naturally.

Emma Oh. Well. When do I start?

Keith When you're ready. I'm getting dressed. You can tell Alistair he's cook for the day.

Emma Cook?

Keith Yes.

Emma Alistair?

Keith Yes.

Emma God. (*She goes down the steps to the saloon*) Won't be a sec.

Vince All right to cast off without you, will it, Skipper?

Keith Yes, carry on, Vince. I'll——

June comes up the steps from their cabin

    Good Lord, what's got you up?
June Someone banging on our roof got me up.
Vince Sorry.
June Good-morning. Thank you for nothing.
Keith (*to Vince, laughing*) You're in the doghouse. Won't be long.

Keith goes into his cabin. June looks around and seeing no-one about, takes Vince's hand and nibbles the finger

Vince (*quietly*) Ow.
June Thank you for waking me up, you bastard.
Vince You didn't sleep very much anyway, did you?
June You heard us, did you?
Vince Certainly did.
June Thought you would.
Vince There's nothing wrong with you, Ginger——
June Mm?
Vince —that a little naval discipline wouldn't put right.
June Lovely.

Emma comes back from the saloon, now in her life-jacket. June moves swiftly to the side of the boat

Emma (*as she comes on deck*) All right.
June (*peering unconvincingly into the water*) Little fishes. Lots and lots of little fishes.
Emma Morning, June.
June Oh, good-morning. Just looking at the little fishes. Wheee.
Emma OK. What do I do?
Vince Right. Stand here. Now, the first thing to remember about a boat as opposed to a car——
June What are you doing?
Emma I'm learning to drive. Vince is teaching me.
June Oh, lovely.
Vince We're all doing different jobs. Different job every day.
June Really? And what are you doing?
Vince Shopping and teaching her.
June I see.
Vince You're on cabin maintenance, by the way.
June What?
Vince Tidying up.
June You're joking.
Vince Don't blame me, take it up with the skipper.
June (*going down the steps to her cabin*) I shall. I do quite enough cabin maintenance at home, thank you very much. (*She goes*)
Vince Now the first thing is to start your engine. Switch on. There's your starter.

The engine roars into life. Vince kills it

Want to try it?
Emma All right.
Vince No. Key first. (*Taking her hand*) Turn that, you see.
Emma Yes.
Vince (*taking her other hand as well*) And then that.

The engine starts

Well done.
Emma Yes. You don't have to do that.
Vince Sorry?
Emma Keep holding on to me. Please don't keep doing that. I can manage, thank you.
Vince What?
Emma Please don't. I don't like it. Thank you.
Vince Beg your pardon. Sorry.
Emma Sorry.
Vince You're safe enough.
Emma Yes, I'm sure.
Vince I'm not going to try anything, you know. Not while you're in that life-jacket.
Emma (*smiling*) Oh—yes . . .

June stomps back on deck

June It seems that I'm doing bloody cabin maintenance whether I like it or not.
Emma We're all doing something.
June So it appears. (*She goes down into the saloon*) Excuse me.

Alistair squeezes past her

Vince (*to Emma*) The thing about handling a boat as opposed to a car is——
Alistair Did you say cooking?
Emma Yes.
Alistair Right. What am I cooking?
Emma Whatever you want?
Vince You're the cook.
Alistair Oh no, I'm not, you know.
Emma Oh no, he's not, you know.
Vince All right. Alistair, can you take the stern line, we're about to cast off. (*Calling into the saloon*) Gingernut.
June (*from within*) What?
Vince Come and help us cast off.
Alistair (*moving astern*) Where's Keith?
June (*coming back on deck*) He's in the shower. You want me to what?

Alistair jumps ashore

Vince Cast off, please. Can you take the bow line.
June Me?
Vince Yes, you.

June God, this is getting worse and worse. It's like one of those awful outward bound things. What do I have to do?

Alistair (*already ashore and helping her off*) Come on, come down. I'll show you what to do. It's quite easy. You untie this, you see . . .

Vince OK, now look. While we're here, I might as well show you the correct way to do this. That is, the correct procedure to employ when leaving a mooring on a river. So the next time we all go into a lock, we'll all know what we're doing. We'll all know what we're talking about. We won't get silly buggers roaring their heads off at us like they did on that bridge yesterday. This is just so you'll know. OK? I take it you've no objection to wanting to know? You'd like to do things properly, wouldn't you?

June Of course we would.

Alistair Yep.

Vince Cookie?

Emma Oh, yes.

Vince (*in the loud, clear voice of an army small arms instructor*) All right. (*He bounds ashore*) Now somebody tell me what I've got in my hand here. (*He holds up the bow line*)

June A piece of rope.

Vince Incorrect. This is not a rope. It maybe what you call a rope but it is not called a rope, not on the river. On the river, it is called a scuff. This I am holding is your bow scuff or fore scuff. The one Alistair is holding is known as your stern scuff.

Alistair I didn't know that.

Vince You will notice, that both your scuffs were attached to a metal ring. This . . . (*he demonstrates*) . . . which we call a piggle.

June A what?

Vince You attach your scuff to your piggle by inserting it through the piggle like so and then tying it off with two half semi-stanchions or sheep shackles. OK? (*He demonstrates as he speaks*)

Alistair Really?

Vince And you do the same there, will you?

Alistair does so

Emma I've never heard of any of this.

Vince Then pay attention, you'll learn something. Now, to the boat itself. This is divided you'll notice into various areas — all of which have names. Now there are the names they print in the brochures for the benefit of the uninitiated and then there are the correct names that any self-respecting boat owner would normally use. So if you don't want to make idiots of yourselves, you'd better learn the proper ones. (*Jumping on to the bow*) This area here is known as your gaff deck. The gaff deck. Immediately below, the area beneath that we refer to as the scuppers. You two are sleeping in the scuppers.

Emma I thought we were.

Vince Moving along — (*he stands on the saloon roof*) — the weevil deck, all right? And beneath that, what *you* call the saloon and *we* call the mizen.

Emma What's the kitchen called then?

Vince It's called the galley, Cookie, you knew that, didn't you? (*Jumping down beside her*) This area here, the so-called cockpit is in fact, your kedge deck. Further astern, stepping on to the roof of the poop cabin — below me is called the poop cabin — this deck area here is the dodger. (*Moving aft again*) And here, right at the very very stern, this area we call the snuffle deck. For obvious reasons. Finally, that narrow corridor running from your snuffle down each side of your dodger, round your kedge, forward again past your weevil and meeting at your gaff are your port and starboard squeezes. They speak for themselves.

June This is terribly confusing.

Vince Soon pick it up, you'll soon pick it up.

Alistair You sure about this?

Vince What's the matter?

Alistair Well, it's just odd that I — well, I've never actually heard any of these ... Well, I've heard of them but not — in these contexts. I mean, weevil and kedge ...

Vince What are you saying?

Alistair Well, I'm saying I've——

Vince No, I'm sorry I don't quite see what you're saying.

Alistair (*backing down*) Well, nothing.

Emma (*who has been hunting around*) Where's that book?

Vince Book?

Emma That one of Keith's. It was here. That will tell us.

Vince You want to check something?

Emma Well, only that ... I'm sure you're right, it's just I don't know where it is.

Vince If it's the one that was here the other day, it's out of date anyway. OK shall we give it a try? Start engines.

Emma does so

Good. Well done, Cookie. All right, when I say go both of you unfasten your scuffs, pull them clear of your piggles and wait for the command to board. All right, off you go as quick as you can.

June on the bow and Alistair on the stern fumble to unfasten their lines

June Oh, God.

Vince Come on, come on, Gingernut.

June All right, all right.

June and Alistair succeed in unfastening their ropes. Alistair starts to board at the stern

Vince Where do you think you're going?

Alistair I'm coming aboard.

Vince Didn't you hear me say wait for the command? Now wait for the command. You go jumping around unilaterally like that, you can confuse your helmsman here and cause a serious incident in a crowded lock.

Alistair Sorry.

Vince This is all based on good common sense. None of this is for show. It's practical. Right. Here comes the command. Bow aboard with your scuff and as soon as you're there, you shout out – "Bow scuff aboard, Skipper". So she can hear you. (*Indicating Emma*)

June Is that me that does that?

Vince Yes. Come on, Ginger, off you go.

June scrambles aboard

Quick as you can.

June (*on board with her rope*) Right, done it.

Vince Good, and what do you say?

June Aboard scuff, Skipper.

Vince No. Bow scuff aboard, Skipper.

June Sorry.

Vince Right. Say it.

June God. Bow scuff aboard, Skipper.

Vince Loudly. She can't hear you, she's got her engine running. Loudly.

June (*loud and angrily*) Bow scuff aboard, Skipper.

Vince That's it. Well done, Ginger. All right. Now.

He turns to see Alistair climbing aboard again

What are you doing now?

Alistair I'm getting on board. The boat's going without me.

Vince What have you got in your hand?

Alistair A rope.

Vince A what?

Alistair A scuff.

Vince What's your scuff attached to?

Alistair The boat. The – snuffle deck.

Vince So if you hold on to that, you'll be all right, won't you? The boat's going nowhere unless you let it. Now on the command, you jump aboard with your scuff and as soon as you're in position, "Stern scuff aboard, Skipper". All right?

Alistair Right.

Vince Off you go, then. Stern aboard.

Alistair clambers aboard

Alistair Stern scuff aboard, Skipper.

Vince Good. Now, your final job is to coil, on the deck, your scuff in a concentric circle of not more than eighteen inches in diameter.

June Oh, come on.

Vince Any larger ring than that constitutes a deck hazard. Which means that it'll be your fault the next time somebody trips over it, falls overboard and is carved up into small pieces by the propeller.

June (*attempting to coil her rope*) Eighteen inches, this'll take all night.

Vince All right, Cookie?

Emma It's fine for me, it's great.

Vince Now, once they're clear you put your engine slow ahead, wheel to port and ease out. (*Calling to the others*) Have you done that?

June No.
Alistair No.
Vince Right, let's start again. Cut engine.

Vince leaves the cockpit, goes forward, takes June's line from her, jumps ashore and ties it off again

June What are we doing?
Vince Alistair, bring your scuff ashore and tie off, please.
Alistair What's happening?
Vince Do it all again. Get it dead right.

Alistair comes ashore

Alistair I've just got my circle.
Vince Come on, if a thing's worth doing, it's worth doing right. What's the deck called?
Emma Er — weevil deck.
Vince That one?
June Gaff. No, gaffer. Gaff.
Vince Gaff, good. What are you standing on?
Emma Oh, hang on, it's like rice and paella. No.
Vince Kedge.
Emma Kedgeree, kedge, yes. You haven't seen that book, have you?
Vince Ready there, now.
June Ready.
Vince Alistair?
Alistair Yes, nearly.
Vince Come on, Alistair. We'll call you Lightning, I think. Lightning Wingate.

June laughs

Alistair OK.
Vince Right. And off we go, and switch on.

Emma does so. June and Alistair untie their knots again

Wait for it, and — bows aboard. Off you go, Ginger.

June scrambles aboard

June (*loudly*) Bow scuff aboard, Skipper.
Vince And stern aboard.

Alistair climbs aboard

Coil your rope, Ginger.
June Oh, yes.
Vince Come on, Lightning.
Alistair Right, I'm here. Oh, er — stern scuff aboard, Skipper.
Vince What?
Alistair Stern scuff aboard, Skipper.
Vince I can't hear him. (*To Emma*) Can you hear him? Louder.

Alistair Stern scuff aboard, Skipper.

Vince Again, louder.

Emma I can hear him.

Vince Come on, again.

Alistair Oh, bugger this. (*He throws down the rope, jumps ashore and sits on the bank*)

Vince All right. We now have a stern scuff ready to tangle round our propeller. Brilliant, Lightning. Good thinking.

Alistair (*muttering*) Look, I'm not coming on holiday — to be bloody shouted at . . . I'm not. I'm sorry.

June Oh, come on, Alistair, don't be so weedy.

Alistair (*quite near to tears*) I'm not bloody . . . Sorry . . . I'm bloody not.

Silence

Vince (*calmly*) Alistair.

Alistair doesn't reply

Alistair.

Alistair Yes.

Vince You want to take over? That what you'd like?

Alistair Oh, get stuffed.

Emma switches off the engine

Emma Wait a minute, wait a minute. (*She gets off the boat and goes to Alistair*)

June I've made a lovely circle. Can I have a gold star, please?

Vince That's two foot six if it's an inch. I said, eighteen inches.

June Oh, really.

Emma (*sitting beside Alistair*) Alistair.

Alistair What?

Emma It's OK. What's wrong?

Alistair It's that berk shouting at us all. Who does he think he is?

Emma I think he's only trying to show us. He means well. He's just a bit loud. He'll be gone soon. Come on.

Alistair What?

Emma Well, you can't just sit there. Please. For me.

Vince Right. I think we'll do it once more, shall we?

June Oh no, we don't.

Vince You haven't got it right yet.

June I've got it right. He's the one who didn't get it right.

Vince So now we've all got to do it again. Off you go.

June This is positively the last time. (*She gets off with her rope and re-ties it*)

Vince Cookie?

Emma (*to Alistair*) Come on, last time.

Vince Lightning ready, is he?

Emma (*rescuing Alistair's stern rope and giving it to him*) Yes. Go on.

June This is quite daft. I've broken a nail doing this.

Alistair is re-tying his rope. Emma returns aboard

Vince Could save your life though. OK on the helm?
Emma Yes, coming.
Vince OK bow scuff?
June Yes.
Vince OK. Stern scuff?
Alistair (*sotto*) Just a minute.
Vince What?
Alistair (*bellowing*) Just a minute!
Vince All right, we're waiting for Lightning. Say when, Lightning.

Keith comes on deck, showered and spruce in his skipper's outfit

Keith What on earth's going on here?
Vince Ah, Skipper. We can have a demonstration for the skipper. We're
    learning to cast off properly, Skipper.
June We're getting brilliant. Some of us are.
Alistair OK.
Vince Right. Lightning's ready. Demonstration for the skipper, let's make it
    a good one. Ready? Start engines.
Emma Start engines. (*She does so*)
Vince Let go.

June and Alistair do so

Keith I say, this is impressive.
Vince Bow aboard.

June clambers aboard

June Bow scuff aboard, Skipper.
Vince Stern aboard.

Alistair climbs aboard

Alistair Stern scuff aboard, Skipper.
Vince Slow ahead, helm.
Emma Slow ahead, helm.
Vince Coil your scuffs and get about your duties. All present and correct,
    Skipper. (*He snaps a salute*)
Keith Wow. Well. Well done.
Vince (*to Emma*) Careful. Not too much till you get in the main stream.
Emma Right.
Keith Like a military operation.
Vince That's how it should be, shouldn't it, Skipper?
Keith Oh yes. Rather. Very impressive.

Alistair goes past them very sulkily

    Well done.

Alistair ignores him and goes below forward

June Weren't we good?
Keith Brilliant.

June He's terrific. He knows everything. Go and have a look at my scuff. It's terribly neat. Exactly eighteen inches, I bet you. Oh well, cabin maintenance calls.

June goes below aft

Keith Her what's very neat?
Vince Her scuff. Her rope. Called a scuff, Skipper.
Keith Is it?
Vince Generally.
Keith Oh. Well, I suppose I'd better do my bit. I can't clean much of the deck while we're moving. Bit dangerous.
Emma You can do the kedge.
Keith The what?
Emma This one. The kedge.
Keith You mean the cockpit.
Vince It's usually called the kedge, Skipper.
Keith Is it?
Vince Normally.
Keith Oh.
Vince You could probably do this and the dodger and possibly even the weevil. But I wouldn't try the squeezes or the gaff till we're stationary.
Keith No, no, you're probably right. OK. (*To Emma*) Do you know where the mop is?
Emma Yes. It's in the cupboard between the mizen and the scuppers.
Keith And the what?
Emma The scuppers.
Keith Ah, righto, yes. (*He goes aft*)
Emma No, scuppers. That way.
Keith Oh yes, the scuppers, of course. (*He goes below*)
Vince (*to Emma*) You're handling her well, Cookie, very well.
Emma Thank you.
Vince (*patting her on the shoulder*) You're going to make a very good helmsman.

Emma swells a little with pride inside her life-jacket. She smiles to herself. Vince stands and takes in the air, also pleased with himself. Unseen by Emma, he picks up the map and studies it

June appears from aft looking bright and busy

June I'm making everything look sparkling.
Vince (*winking at her*) Good on you, Ginger.

June blows him a swift furtive kiss and goes down into the saloon

Vince folds the map and tucks it away inside his shirt

Keith comes back on deck from the saloon with the bucket and the mop

Keith Found them.
Vince Well done, Skipper. Here let me.

Vince takes the bucket and leans over the side of the cockpit to fill it with water. Keith meanwhile hunts around Emma

Emma What's the matter?
Keith Have you seen my book? That book of mine?
Emma I don't know, we were just looking.
Keith I couldn't find it yesterday, either.
Vince (*putting bucket on "dodger"*) There you go, Skip.
Keith (*preparing to climb on to the aft deck*) Well, I'll start up here.
Vince Carry on, Skipper.

Keith climbs on to the aft deck and starts mopping uncertainly. Pause

Emma What's that bird there?
Vince It's a guillemot.
Emma A guillemot?
Vince Yes.
Emma I didn't know you found them on rivers.
Vince You find guillemots everywhere. They go where the food is.
Emma Do you recognize a lot of birds?
Vince Most of them. I should do. I was warden on a bird sanctuary for three years.
Emma Where's that map . . .?
Vince (*seeing Keith's ineffectual efforts*) Come on, Skip, give it some elbow.
Keith It's quite tricky up here.

Vince vaults on to the deck and takes the mop from Keith

Vince (*demonstrating vigorously*) Here. Like this. Really scrub at it. You want to get every scrap of mud off. Like this, see?
Keith Yes, yes.
Vince Give it all you've got, Skip.
Keith Yes, I will.

Vince jumps down, leaving Keith scrubbing furiously. June emerges from the saloon. She is amused to see Keith. She starts polishing the saloon doors. Alistair comes on deck briefly with a full washing-up bowl, which he empties over the side. In all, the image is of a very busy boat. Only Vince seems to have time on his hands. He stands centre of the cockpit, master of all he surveys.

Mrs Hatfield appears on the bank. She is dressed more practically and somewhat less formally than before

Mrs Hatfield (*in the distance*) Hallo. Hallo.
Vince Is that your friend there?
Emma Where?
Vince There to starboard.
Mrs Hatfield Hallo.
Emma Oh yes. Keith, it's Mrs Hatfield.
Keith Mrs—? Are we at Slippey already?
Vince No, five miles yet.
Mrs Hatfield Hallo. Emergency.

Keith What's she saying?
Mrs Hatfield Help. Hallo. Emergency.
June Sounds like emergency.
Keith Oh, my God. Right. We'd better get ready to moor.
Vince Ay ay, Skipper. (*Yelling*) All hands on deck for mooring. Come on, let's have you.

Alistair comes up from the saloon

Alistair What's that?
June (*moving forward to the bow*) Oh dear, here we go again.
Vince Stand by your scuffs.

Alistair makes his way to the stern

Hold your course full ahead, helmsman.
Emma Full ahead.

Keith, meanwhile, drops down into the cockpit again bringing his bucket and mop with him

Keith Someone else will have to finish that.
Vince You carry on, Skip.
Keith I'll get my jacket. (*He goes below aft*)
Vince Slow ahead.
Emma Slow ahead.
Mrs Hatfield I'm so sorry, I needed to catch you as soon as possible.
June Problems?
Mrs Hatfield I'm afraid so. I've been chasing you up the river.
June I love that.
Mrs Hatfield What?
June Your outfit. Lovely.
Vince Slow astern.
Emma Slow astern.
June Are there any piggles there, Mrs Hatfield?
Vince That's it. That's enough.
Mrs Hatfield Pardon, any what?
June Piggles. Little iron rings.
Mrs Hatfield Oh, yes, yes, there are. Are they called piggles?
Vince (*to Mrs Hatfield*) Stand clear, please, madam. (*To his crew*) Stand by your scuffs to make fast. And make fast forward.

June jumps ashore

Make fast aft.

Alistair jumps ashore

Stop engines.
Emma Stop engines.
Vince Switch off.
Emma Switch off.
Vince Don't forget to tie off with two sheep shackles.

Mrs Hatfield Very impressive.
June We're getting frightfully good.
Mrs Hatfield So I see. New skipper, is it?
Keith (*coming on deck*) No.
June Don't say that.
Keith What's this, Mrs Hatfield? Did you say emergency?
Mrs Hatfield Yes. May I—(*a glance at Vince*)—may I come aboard?
Keith Yes, of course.
Vince (*offering Mrs Hatfield a hand*) Allow me.
Mrs Hatfield Thank you.
June I hope this business is settled soon. It is hardly a holiday for anyone.
Mrs Hatfield I'm so sorry. I'm so very sorry ...
Keith Come below, come below.

Mrs Hatfield goes into the saloon

Keith You want to join us, Alistair?
Alistair (*who is gloomily sitting on the bank by his rope*) No, thanks.
Keith It's your firm as well, you know. I thought you might be interested. (*He goes below into the saloon*)
June (*climbing back aboard*) I don't think Alistair is interested in anything.
Emma It's odd about that map.
Vince Well, I think I'll take this opportunity to do the shopping.
Emma Shall I give you a list?
Vince It would be very helpful, Cookie, thank you.
Emma I'll check the stores. If I dare interrupt. (*She goes down the steps to the saloon*) Excuse me, sorry.

June is left more or less alone with Vince for a moment

June Presumably you'll need some money.
Vince Presumably.
June Well, you'd better wait there, hadn't you? And if you're good and well-behaved, I'll give you some.

June goes into her cabin. Vince remains inscrutable

Vince (*calling to Alistair*) What are you cooking up for us tonight, Lightning?
Alistair Stew.
Vince Delicious. Isn't that a long business making a stew?
Alistair Only if the tin-opener jams.
Vince Ah.
Emma (*returning from the galley*) We're fairly well stocked up actually. I did some yesterday. Eggs, bread and milk, that's all. Unless you see any decent cheese. Strong Cheddar or something. Can you remember that?
Vince I can remember that, Cookie.
Emma Have you got any money?
June (*coming on deck with her purse*) I'm just sorting him out. (*To Emma*) What's happening in there?
Emma It sounds very heavy.

June Oh, God. Now, how much do you need? Is thirty pounds enough?
Emma Thirty quid! He's only getting a few eggs.
June Well, he might see something else he likes.
Emma He doesn't want thirty quid. Don't be so stupid.
June Just in case.
Emma He's not going to spend thirty quid.
June He can take it just in case. There you are. (*She hands the notes to Vince*)
Vince Thank you kindly, Ginger.
June Why not? I trust him.
Emma It's not a question of that.
June Isn't it?
Emma Of course not.
Vince I'm very trustworthy, Cookie. That's my problem. That's what's made me a victim of the system. See you later.

He jumps ashore and jogs off up the towpath

They watch him

Emma Honestly. Thirty quid.
June It's my thirty quid, I'll do what I like with it.

June goes back to her cabin. As she does so, Keith comes back on deck, grim-faced, followed by Mrs Hatfield

Keith It looks as if I'm going to have to go back.
Emma Oh no.
June (*emerging from her cabin*) For how long?
Keith Just till this evening, I've got to sort it out. It's all getting too much for Martin Cook, quite obviously.
June Is it serious?
Keith Looks like we've got a strike.
June A strike?
Keith Called from two o'clock this afternoon.
Emma Oh, no.
Keith Unless the management are prepared to stand down.
June What nonsense.
Keith Biggest order period of the year and they choose to strike.
June Oh, the bastards.
Keith Well.
June It's the ingratitude that gets me. The sheer ingratitude of these people.
Keith I know, I know.
June My God, they'd be unemployed but for us.
Keith I know, I know.

Keith climbs ashore and helps Mrs Hatfield to do the same

June Don't they realize that? (*To Alistair*) They've called a strike, you know.
Alistair Ah.
June That's if you're in the least concerned.
Mrs Hatfield This is why I had to catch you early, you see.

Keith Quite right, Mrs Hatfield, you did right.
Mrs Hatfield In order to be back by two, you see.
Keith Quite.
Mrs Hatfield Because after that, of course, I'm afraid I'm out as well.
Keith What's that?
Mrs Hatfield I'll be on strike as well. It's unanimous, you see.
Keith You'll be on strike?
June Don't be ridiculous, Mrs Hatfield. You're one of us.
Mrs Hatfield No, technically, Mrs Taylor, I'm actually one of them.
Keith Well, there you are. I now feel I've been stabbed in the back by everyone.
Mrs Hatfield I'm really very sorry it's come to this.
Keith What the hell are you wearing anyway?
Mrs Hatfield Wearing?
Keith Are those the clothes you'd normally expect to wear in the office?
Mrs Hatfield No, well, this is rather an exceptional——
Keith Would you kindly in future come dressed for the job you're paid for and not disguised as some renegade garage mechanic.
Mrs Hatfield (*tight-lipped*) Yes, Mr Taylor.

Mrs Hatfield goes off along the bank

Keith I'll leave Vince in charge. Tell him he's responsible. (*To Alistair*) There's no point in leaving you in charge, is there?
Alistair Nope.
Keith I'll have something to say to you when I get back. You're a broken reed, man, a broken reed.

Keith goes off

June It makes me want to despair of human nature, it really does. I despair.

June goes back to her cabin

Emma (*to Alistair*) You're not going with him, I take it.
Alistair I don't think I'd be very much use.
Emma Well, you might be able to do something.
Alistair The trouble is I can see both their points of view.
Emma Isn't that a good thing?
Alistair Not in this case. It means they wouldn't listen to me, anyway. The only people who get heard in this world are the extremists. They're the only ones with the energy to shout loud enough.
Emma Wonderful. Just wonderful.

It's a hot afternoon, she takes off her life-jacket. Alistair tosses pebbles into the river. June comes back on deck equipped to sun herself. She goes to lie in her familiar spot

June (*sniffing the air suspiciously*) I think he's parked us near the glue works.
Emma Oh, yes?

Emma picks up Keith's discarded mop and starts to tackle the cockpit floor

June I'm going to have a nap before Vince gets back and decides to have keel-hauling practice.

Emma (*smiling*) I think he made half those names up, you know. I can't believe I'm mopping the kedge for a moment.

June What about me? I'm lying on the weevil.

Emma Anyway, he's livened things up.

June Thank God for that.

A silence. Emma mops. June lies on deck. Alistair snoozes on the bank

In a moment or so, Vince returns along the towpath. He carries a cardboard crate full of wine bottles. He is followed by Fleur, a young girl dressed in similar vein to Vince. She carries a bag with more bottles and a small roll of personal belongings. Around her neck, somewhat incongruously, are a pair of very good binoculars

Vince Hi. Skipper tells me he's been called away.

Emma Yes. (*Seeing Fleur*) Oh, hallo.

Vince Guess who I met? My very good friend, that's who I met.

Emma Oh. How very nice.

June (*sitting up*) Oh.

Vince This is Fleur.

Fleur Hi.

Vince This is Emma known as Cookie. This is June known as Ginger and that's Alistair known as Lightning. This is Fleur also known as the Amazing Birdwoman.

June Hallo, then.

Alistair (*without moving*) Hallo.

Emma What have you bought, for goodness sake?

Vince I thought we might all like to celebrate. I bought some grog.

June Grog?

Vince Well, Médoc, Chablis, Sauterne, Château Pumpernickel, that sort of grog. Whatever that little shop sold. (*He dumps his box on the deck*)

Emma Did you get the eggs?

Vince Nor I did.

Emma The bread? Milk?

Vince Damn. I knew there was something else. (*He takes the carrier bag from Fleur and puts it on board*)

Emma How much booze have you bought?

Vince How much money did you give me?

June Thirty pounds.

Vince That's what it must have cost me.

Emma looks at June

June (*laughing bravely*) Super. Well spent.

Vince I thought you'd approve.

Fleur has wandered a little way off along the bank. She is looking at something through her binoculars

Fleur Ah.

Vince What is it?

Fleur It's a grebe.

June A what?

Fleur Grebe. A crested grebe.

Vince I told you, she's the birdwoman. (*He vaults aboard and picks up the crate*) Everything OK?

Emma Who is she?

Vince Friend of mine. You make a lot of friends on the river. (*He goes down into the saloon with the crate*)

Fleur (*to herself*) Lovely bird. It's a lovely, lovely bird.

June (*sotto, to Emma*) What's going on?

Emma (*shrugging*) I don't know.

Vince returns on deck for the carrier

Vince (*shouting*) Hey, Fleur.

Fleur (*groaning as her grebe vanishes*) Don't do that, Vince.

Vince Come on, we're having a party.

June Wait a minute. Who says we're having a party?

Vince Listen, Ginger, we've got nothing to do with ourselves, have we, till the skipper gets back. Can't move the boat. We can't leave it. So we might as well have a party. Fleur! (*He goes below with the carrier*)

Fleur Coming. (*She climbs on board*)

June and Emma watch her

(*To them*) Hi. He's always having parties. (*She goes below to the saloon*)

June With other people's money, presumably. Oh well.

Emma (*smiling*) Oh well.

They both go down into the saloon

Time passes again. Jollities get under way. Glasses, bottles opening and laughter. Darkness falls. The saloon lights come on. As this is happening, Alistair comes nearer and climbs aboard. He sits aft on the cabin roof. Some James Last music is heard from the cassette recorder below. In time, Fleur emerges with a glass

Fleur Hallo.

Alistair Hallo.

Fleur Don't you like parties, then?

Alistair Well, sometimes.

Fleur You've been sitting up here for hours, haven't you? I've been watching you.

Alistair Oh.

Fleur I'm Fleur,

Alistair Yes. Hallo.

Fleur I'm a friend of Vince's.

Alistair Yes.

Fleur You should come down. There's all us women and just Vince. It's terrible.

Alistair I'm sure he can manage.

Fleur How do you mean?

Alistair I'm sure Vince can keep three women happy with no problems.

Fleur Oh well, yes. With Vince, it's the more the merrier. I've had twosomes, and threesomes and foursomes and fivesomes. So many people in one bed. Actually, it can be very unhygienic. Are you interested in birdwatching?

Alistair Bird—well, I don't know much about them, I'm afraid.

Fleur Well, I didn't either. I got these binoculars, you know, from a tenant who couldn't pay his rent. And it's opened a whole new world. You get incredibly hooked. I mean, seeing that grebe earlier has just made the day. Of course, what I'm really after is the kingfisher. That's, of course, the ultimate.

Alistair Oh.

Fleur I've seen this heron two or three times and that was tremendous. But it's the kingfisher really. That has got to be the river bird really. It's just unbelievable. Are you married to Ginger or the other one?

Alistair The other one. To Emma.

Fleur Yes, I thought you would be.

Alistair Why?

Fleur I don't know. You look—suited.

Alistair What do you do?

Fleur When?

Alistair For a living.

Fleur Nothing to speak of.

Alistair Oh, you're unemployed, are you?

Fleur No, I'm very rich really. I've got a lot of property and I let that to people at vast rents so I don't have to worry.

Alistair Oh.

Fleur (*smiling*) Capitalist, you see.

Alistair Ah.

Fleur My father's incredibly rich. He's the richest person I know.

Alistair Great.

Fleur It's the only way to be really, isn't it? (*Studying him*) You look very unhappy, you know. You ought to drink some of this.

Alistair I don't think I——

Fleur Go on.

Alistair I get very ill after two glasses.

Fleur Well, only have one. (*Offering her glass*) Here.

Alistair (*drinking*) Very good.

Fleur Vince bought it. He may have no money but he's got the most amazing taste. It's a lethal mixture.

Alistair Excellent. Thank you.

Fleur Have it all. (*Smiling*) I'm not trying to get you drunk.

Alistair (*smiling back*) Fair enough. (*He drinks again*)

Fleur Would you—would you like to dance with me?

Alistair Oh, no, I don't.

Fleur Come on.

Alistair Well, I never really ... No, thanks.

Fleur Please. Please. I would love to. I would like very much to dance with you.
Alistair Why?
Fleur I just would.
Alistair I can't dance.
Fleur I don't care. Neither can I.
Alistair Oh, I——
Fleur (*enticingly*) Come on.
Alistair Well.
Fleur Please. (*She holds her hand out*)
Alistair (*allowing himself to be led to the middle of the cockpit*) OK. I'm not — I'm no good at all.
Fleur Well, it's draggy music anyway, isn't it?
Alistair I think it's Keith's.
Fleur It doesn't sound like something you'd listen to. Hey, you're a terrific dancer.

Emma comes up from the saloon with a glass of wine

Emma Well, well.
Fleur (*pushing Alistair away*) There you are, you see. You owe me a pound.
Emma Yes, all right.
Alistair What?
Emma I bet her she'd never get you to dance with her. She's won. I've lost.
Fleur It wasn't difficult at all.
Alistair Ah. (*He sits on the side of the deck again*)

June comes up on deck with her glass, a little hot and flustered from Vince's attention. The music stops

June This is the place to be. On deck. (*Sotto, to Emma*) You left me down there on my own with him.
Emma (*shrugging*) Sorry.
Vince (*coming on deck with a bottle*) We have decided, in view of the lack of any decent music on your cassette machine, that we're going to make our own. We are very fortunate to have to entertain us the one and only June Gingernut, who's gladly consented to give us some of her best known numbers.
Emma Has she?
June She's going to try.
Fleur Hooray.
June Wait a minute. Wait a minute. I need a costume. I can't be a Gingernut without a costume.
Vince You travel your costume?
June No, no. Something like it. I'll find something like it. It's a hoot. You'll love it. (*She hurries into her cabin*)

The aft cabin lights come on

Vince Hallo, Lightning.

Alistair Hallo.

Vince Give Lightning a glass.

Alistair No.

Emma Oh, come on, Alistair, just for once enjoy yourself. Have a drink. Here, take it.

Alistair You know what'll happen.

Emma Yes, I know what'll happen.

Vince Come on, Gingernut, what are we waiting for?

Fleur Get 'em off.

June (*from below*) Just a minute.

Vince Isn't this a terrific party, Cookie?

Emma It's a terrific party, Vince.

Vince puts an arm round Emma's shoulder. She does not resist. With his other hand, he strokes the top of Fleur's head. Alistair sits apart, sipping his wine like cough medicine

Alistair Fleur was telling me she's very rich.

Emma Is she?

Vince She's incredibly rich. She's a daughter of a duke, you know.

Emma Are you?

Fleur He's an earl, not a duke. You always get it wrong.

Vince Beg his pardon. He's an earl. She's Lady something, aren't you?

Fleur Lady Catherine Elizabeth Lucy Sadler Fleur. How about that? Impressive, eh?

Emma Terribly. I'm just Emma Fay.

Fleur Oh, poor thing. Well, have one of mine. Feel free.

Emma Thank you.

June's head appears coyly over the top of the aft cabin doors

June Now, listen.

Vince, Emma and Fleur all cheer and applaud

Vince Bravo, bring on the Gingers.

June Now, listen, listen. You're going to have to use your imaginations a bit.

Vince Shame.

Emma Rubbish.

Fleur Cobblers.

June You've got to imagine I'm seventeen.

Vince Yahoo!

Emma Oh, dear.

June All right. Ready?

June disappears and then almost immediately re-enters with a big theatrical entrance. She wears Keith's captain's hat and a make-shift costume which places her somewhere between Shirley Temple and Sally Bowles. The impact is decidedly bizarre. A great deal of whooping and cheering as June, providing her own musical accompaniment, shimmies on to the deck

(*Singing*)

Introducing those Gingernuts
Four fresh baked Gingernuts
Four kids who badly want to sing you
Numbers that will bring you
Memories
Full of laughter
With maybe
A tear.
Here come those Gingernuts
I'm Gingernut June—hallo—
Tippy-tapping a tune
Doopy-doopy-doo-doo
With brothers Robin and Roy
And my wee sister Joy.
Introducing those Gingernuts . . .

The song has taken her via some creaky choreography on to the aft cabin roof. Alistair stares incredulously. Emma, after initial embarrassment at seeing her friend make quite such a fool of herself, is reduced to helpless hysterics. Fleur and Vince whoop and cat-call.

Just as June is about to re-start the whole awful performance again, Keith arrives along the towpath. He's obviously had a terrible time. He stares at June in horror

Keith (*a fierce bellow*) June!
June (*stopping*) Oh, he's back.
Keith What are you doing? What the hell are you doing?
June Cabaret time.
Keith What are you playing at? I could hear you from the middle of the village.
June Oh, was it loud?
Keith Loud? There were about fifty people watching you from the pub car park.
June (*pleased*) Oh, really?
Emma (*giggling*) We could pass a hat round.
Keith What is going on here? What's going on?
Vince Just a little party, Skipper.
Keith You're all drunk out of your heads.
Fleur Would you like a drink?
Keith Who the hell's this?
Vince This is a friend of mine. Fleur, this is Mr——
Keith June, will you put some bloody clothes on, please.
June Oh, come on, Keith, we were having a bit of fun, that's all.
Keith Fun?
Vince She was showing us her Gingernuts, Skip.

Emma goes off into peals of laughter

Keith (*to Vince*) That's quite enough from you.

June Oh, come on, Keith, don't you remember? (*Singing*) Introducing those Gingernuts ...

Keith Listen, June, I have not had a good day. In fact, I have had the worst day of my life. I have had the truly exhilarating experience of finding myself locked out of my own factory by my own employees. I have spent four hours this afternoon with my face pressed up against a wire fence, attempting to negotiate with Ray Duffy. I am tired, I am angry and I am frustrated. The last thing I want is to come back to witness the spectacle of my wife prancing around half-naked on the roof of a rented boat making a complete and utter bloody idiot of herself in front of an audience of two hundred sniggering strangers. Now will you get down from there at once. You are pathetic and embarrassing.

June (*livid*) How dare you speak to me like that? How dare you, you despicable little man.

Vince Easy on, Skipper.

Keith And you are off this boat as of now.

Vince Pardon?

Keith Off. You and her, whoever she is. Off. Both of you.

Emma Now, just a minute, she's an earl's daughter.

Keith I've got his number. I've got his number. Off.

June Just what right have you got to order people around like that?

Keith I'm not arguing. That's it. Off. (*He goes down into the aft cabin*)

June growls with frustration

Vince Ah well, Fleur. Time to go.

Emma Where are you off to?

Vince Skipper says we have to go, we have to go.

June Nonsense.

Vince He's the skipper. Rule of the river. Abide by the skipper.

Emma Oh come on, Vince, don't take any notice of Keith.

Vince You heard him. He asked us to leave.

June Well, we're asking you to stay. Now, sit down.

Vince No, listen. Let me explain. You're a crew. And you've elected a certain person as your skipper. Now as a result, that man is fully within his rights to order anyone he wants off his boat.

June Elected? We didn't elect him.

Vince Didn't you?

June Of course not. He just took over. Like he does with everything.

Emma We certainly didn't elect him.

Vince Well ... none the less ...

Emma He's no more right to the title than anyone else. Alistair and I have paid for half of this. We're just as entitled to be called skippers.

Vince Ah, yes, but you can't have four skippers, can you? Someone's got to be in charge.

June Well, we ought to elect somebody then. Let's do that.

Emma Let's.

Keith emerges again

Keith June, are you coming to bed?

June Wait a moment.

Keith What?

June We're electing a skipper. We feel it's about time we had one.

Keith What the hell are you talking about?

June There's his hat. It's up for grabs. (*She tosses Keith's cap into the middle of the cockpit*)

Keith Don't do that with it.

June Ah-ah, don't pick it up. Not till you've been elected. Do you wish to be considered for election?

Keith I don't need to be elected. That's my hat. Now, get off this boat.

June Keith would like to be considered. Any more candidates? Emma? Alistair? . . . Well, I would like to propose Vince as skipper.

Vince (*appalled by the suggestion*) Oh, now . . .

Keith Vince? What are you talking about?

June I am proposing Vince.

Keith Now, listen, don't you start this . . .

June All those in favour of Keith as skipper, could we have a show of hands, please?

Keith I'm warning you, June . . . you push this any further and I'm leaving this boat with you on it, here and now. I've had quite enough of this today.

June Any votes for Keith? No? You know, I don't think anyone's voting for you at all, Keith.

Vince I vote for the skipper. I'll stick with the skipper.

Keith Thank you very much indeed.

Vince He's the man for me.

June Now, votes for Vince. Any votes for Vince?

Emma, June and Fleur put up their hands

Well, that looks like it. Vince is our skipper.

Keith Oh no, he isn't. He doesn't even have a legal right to be here.

June Oh, don't start all that again. It was a fair vote and you've been defeated. Now behave like a gentleman and accept it.

Vince It did look rather unanimous, Keith.

Keith It didn't at all. I got your vote, didn't I? (*Pointing to Alistair*) What about him? What about his? He'll vote for me, won't you?

Emma Alistair?

Alistair Mm?

Emma Do you want to vote for Keith?

Alistair (*who is feeling the effect of his two glasses of wine rather*) Well. Yes. And no. Really.

Keith Oh, my God, I should have known better.

June Well, congratulations to our new skipper. We can't kick you off the boat now, can we? (*She hands him the skipper's hat*)

Vince Well, very reluctantly . . .

Keith I am not accepting this, you know. I'm not accepting it. Tomorrow morning I am bringing in the law. (*He goes downstairs aft*)

June (*raising her glass*) To the new skipper.

Emma
Fleur }(*together*) The skipper.

Vince Well, thank you, I'm——
Fleur Speech.
Vince I'll—do my best. If it's still your general intention to go all the way upstream ...
June Of course.
Vince I promise to get you to Armageddon Bridge in one piece. And possibly even back again.
June Bravo.

She leads the clapping from all but Alistair

Keith returns on deck with his briefcase into which he is jamming one or two toilet items

Keith This will not rest here. Not by a long chalk it won't.
Emma Where are you going?
Keith I'm going along to that hotel. And I'm staying the night there.
June If you can get in.
Keith Then I'll look until I do find somewhere.
June Don't be so childish.
Alistair Keith, I don't think you should go rushing off like this, you know.
Keith (*turning on him savagely*) Don't you talk to me. I don't want to hear anything from you. You've given me no support. Nothing. Not at the factory. Not here. We're through. That's it. Partnership dissolved. Friendship dissolved. (*He climbs out of the boat*)
Emma Oh, Keith, no.
Keith (*moving off up the river bank*) This is mutiny, you know. It is legally mutiny. Deposing a captain of a ship against his will is mutiny. I'll be back in the morning.

Keith goes off along the bank

Alistair I honestly don't feel—we should have—should have let him go. I mean, he's not a bad bloke really, he's ... (*He tails away*)
June Oh, shut up, you great soggy lump of nothing. (*She goes down into her cabin*)
Alistair Is she talking to me?
Emma Yes.
Alistair Yes. Thought she was. Well, excuse me, I'm a little bit—a little bit ... excuse me. (*He makes it with difficulty to the gangway*) Night-night. (*He goes down into the saloon*)
Emma He's only had two glasses. Oh well, I suppose I better help him. (*She follows him down*)

The forward cabin lights come on. Vince, still in his captain's hat, surveys his new craft, well pleased

Fleur It was just this sensational view of this grebe. I've never got that close to one. I could almost touch it. Seeing it through the glasses, it was about an inch from me. Amazing.
Vince I told you they were great glasses. Wasn't that a nice present I gave you?
Fleur Oh, Vince, lovely. They're the nicest rent I've ever had from anybody.

A loud sob from June in the aft cabin. Vince and Fleur ignore it

Did you say we were going upstream?
Vince Right.
Fleur Good. I can look for that kingfisher.

Another sob from June

Vince I'd better go and cheer up my crew. (*He gets up and collects the bottle and two glasses*)
Fleur Have a good time.
Vince Right.

Another sob from June

Fleur Hey, would you mind telling me where I fit in to this jolly little crew?
Vince First mate.
Fleur Oh, goodie.
Vince (*rummaging around in the cockpit locker*) Come and join us in twenty minutes.
Fleur Oh, Vince, no.
Vince (*producing a coil of rope*) I'll teach her some knots. They're useful things for sailors to know about.

Vince goes aft. From aft, a laugh from Vince and a feigned cry of surprise from June

Fleur wrinkles her nose distastefully, and moves forward away from the sounds. As she does so, the forward cabin lights go off and in a moment or so the aft cabin lights. Fleur sits in the prow gazing at the river. A squawk from June and a laugh from Vince. The boat rocks gently

Alistair comes out from the saloon, still feeling rather ill and in need of air. He goes to the side of the cockpit and steadies himself. Fleur watches him

Alistair (*seeing her*) Ah.
Fleur Hi.

Further laughs from Vince and June

Alistair Are they—er . . .?
Fleur Yes.
Alistair Oh. Oh, dear.
Fleur Don't you approve?
Alistair (*climbing up to join her*) Well, at the end of it, you know, I don't really know, you know. (*Pause*) No. Which in my case is par for the course. Except that I wish they'd be a bit quieter about it. (*Pause*) He's obviously quite a man, isn't he, Vince? I mean, there he is. June downstairs, you waiting upstairs. I think Emma's even a little bit—taken with him . . .
Fleur He's very positive. They're always attractive, positive people.
Alistair Ah, well. Obviously I'm not a very positive person.
Fleur Emma must have thought you were.
Alistair Ah. Emma, yes. I think she realizes now she made a terrible mistake. It's not that I don't want to be positive, it's just that—well, even when I

have positive ideas, dreams if you like, I tend to be unable to express them
anyway. (*Smiling*) I mean, I was sitting here with Emma just a few nights
ago, and I was trying to tell her some crazy notion I'd had which I thought
might make her happy. I know it would have made her happy. Only I
couldn't say it. I don't think it was embarrassment but — I just couldn't say
it. Silly.

Fleur What was it? Your notion?

Alistair Oh, the notion. Well — you see, I can tell you, there's no problem
with you — I had this thought that, one day, Emma and I would take a boat
on our own and go up the river together, way upstream where it was really
deserted and . . . we'd find a really quiet bit with just a few of those tiny
islands, you know, and one baking hot afternoon, we'd both dive off the
boat — without any clothes on, you know . . .

Fleur Naked . . .

Alistair Yes, naked. And we'd swim around a bit and then we'd chance on
one of these islands and we'd crawl ashore on to the grass, in the rushes,
and we'd, er — you know . . .

Fleur Make love.

Alistair That's it. You see, I can say it to you, a complete stranger. It's easy.

Fleur It's a nice notion. You should have told her. She'd've liked it.

Alistair Well, no. I don't think she'd have been very interested really.

Fleur Why not?

Alistair She can't swim.

Fleur You could lifesave her. Do you know how to do that? She floats on her
back in the water——

Alistair Uh-huh.

Fleur —and you lie on your back underneath her——

Alistair Mm. Mm.

Fleur —then you slip your arms under her arms——

Alistair I get it. Yes, I get it.

Fleur —and then you hold her here with one arm——

Alistair Yes, yes.

Fleur —and with your other hand, you just gently cup under her chin——

Alistair Ah.

Fleur —and that way she feels very safe and helpless, but not at all
frightened.

Alistair No. (*Pause. He laughs*)

Fleur (*smiling*) I don't think you're a negative man at all. Not at all.

Alistair laughs again

All right. (*She stands up*)

Alistair Um?

Fleur Want to give it a try?

Alistair What?

Fleur A swim. Coming for a swim? (*She starts to unfasten her clothes*)

Alistair Hang on.

Fleur What?

Alistair Don't do that. Please.

Fleur Oh, now you have gone negative.

Alistair No, I haven't. Actually, I think I'm going positive. Please don't take this the wrong way, will you, but it sort of has to be with Emma, you see. I mean, you're terribly attractive and nice ... oh, God.

Fleur But it has to be with Emma.

Alistair Yes.

Fleur OK. Fine. No more to say then, is there? Good-night, then.

Alistair (*rising*) Sorry.

Fleur Good-night.

Alistair Good-night. (*He retreats to the saloon doors*) Er—I hope you haven't lost your bet this time, have you?

Fleur scowls. Alistair goes into the saloon and closes the door. A second later, Vince's head appears through the aft hatch

Vince (*an urgent whisper*) Fleur. Fleur.

Fleur Yes?

Vince Come on, where the hell are you?

Fleur Coming.

Vince Quick. I need help.

The hatch shuts

> *Fleur moves along the boat to join them. Somewhere, ashore, in the darkness a nightbird sings. Fleur stops to listen. The bird repeats its call. Fleur jumps ashore and wanders off slowly into the darkness in search of it*

> *Dawn of day six on the river. Unlike its predecessors, a grey unpromising day. Vince comes up on deck. He makes no concessions to the drop in temperature*

> (*Doing his usual early morning round*) Come on, let's be having you. Good-morning, good-morning. All hands on deck. Come on, you idle bunch.

June, amazingly, comes springing out of her cabin in a smart track suit and trim little hat

June (*brightly*) Right, I'm here. Don't know about anybody else but I'm here.

Vince Well done, Gingernut. You've had a slightly unfair advantage over the others but never mind.

Emma comes on deck from the saloon

Emma Good-morning. Isn't this a dreary day?

June I know, it's been so nice up to now.

Vince Now, we're not going to let a little grey weather depress us, are we? Come on, come on.

Alistair blunders on deck

> *Also during the next Fleur wanders back from her morning walk, binoculars in hand and goes below into the saloon*

Alistair Oh God, it gets earlier and earlier.

Vince We want to be off, Lightning, I don't know about you.

Alistair With no breakfast?

Vince You'll get that on the move. Now, we lost valuable time yesterday. We've got to make it up today. We need to do at least thirty miles.

Emma Thirty miles?

Vince At least. Fleur.

Fleur (*from below*) What?

Vince On deck, you idle birdwatcher.

Fleur (*looking out of the saloon*) Hi.

Vince Right. Duties for the day. Fleur at the helm, please. Gingernut, deck maintenance.

June Oh, really.

Vince If you please.

June It's terribly chilly for that.

Vince Lightning, cabin maintenance.

Alistair Right.

Vince Cookie?

Emma Yes.

Vince In the galley.

Emma Oh, really?

Vince That's where I'd like you.

Emma I was rather hoping I'd——

Vince What?

Emma I'd be able to do something else. I mean, I thought we were moving round——

Vince We are, Cookie, but we're moving in a mysterious way as the hymn book would have it.

Emma Well, I don't want to be stuck——

Vince Cookie?

Emma Yes.

Vince I tell you what, if you don't want to pull your weight on this boat, that's fine but in that case, it wouldn't be fair, would it, to expect this boat to pull your weight. So if you'd like a little walk along the towpath today, just say the word and we'll drop you off.

Emma (*looking and receiving no support from the others*) Oh, I see. Well, terrific. OK, it looks as if I'm in the galley then. But it had better not be tomorrow as well. (*She starts down the saloon steps*)

Vince Cookie. Shall we get in the habit of saying skipper, shall we? Don't want to get sloppy, do we?

Emma No, Skipper.

Vince Right. Stand by your scuffs fore and aft.

June and Alistair jump ashore

(*To Fleur*) Handle this, can you?

Fleur Piece of piss.

Vince Start engines.

Fleur Start engines, Skipper.

The engine starts

Vince Ready on your scuffs.
June Ready on the bow scuff, Skipper.
Alistair Just a second, just a second.
Vince Come on, Lightning. Half rations tonight, if you don't move faster
  than that.
Alistair Ready on the stern scuff, Skipper.
Vince Let go forward.
June Let go forward, Skipper. (*She jumps aboard*)
Vince Let go aft.
Alistair Let go aft, Skipper. (*He jumps aboard*)
June Bow scuff aboard, Skipper.
Alistair Stern scuff aboard, Skipper.
Vince Ease her out.
Fleur Ease her out, Skipper.
Vince All right. Coil your scuffs and go about your duties.

June coils her rope and comes down to the cockpit. Alistair does the same

  Get that breakfast started, Cookie.
Emma (*coolly from below*) That's what I'm doing, Skipper.
Vince Slow ahead now.
Fleur Slow ahead, Skipper.
Vince (*to Fleur*) Call me if anything happens.
Fleur Right, Skipper.

Vince goes below into the saloon

June (*pausing to watch Fleur*) You seem to know what you're doing. With
  the boat.
Fleur Thank you.
June You've driven one before?
Fleur Yes, my father's got one. Forty-two foot convertible. Twin-screw.
  Flying bridge. Beauty.
June On the Orb, is it? Or the Thames?
Fleur Bermuda.
June Oh, super.

Fleur sees someone on the bank in the distance

Fleur (*shouting down into the saloon*) Something coming up, Skipper.

Vince comes on deck

Vince What?
Fleur (*pointing*) Look.

  Keith appears on the bank in the distance. He waves

Keith (*jovially*) Good-morning.
Vince Slow ahead.
Fleur Slow ahead, Skipper.
Keith Well, I don't know about you but Keith Taylor had an excellent night
  at a very reasonable hotel. He had a first-class breakfast. Kidneys and
  bacon and delicious fried bread.

Emma comes on deck

Good-morning to you all. So all in all, Keith Taylor is happy to look on last night as a momentary lapse in an otherwise perfect holiday. True, his business is in ruins, his workers are even now looting and pillaging inside his factory — apparently with the full blessing of the law — but none the less, he is not going to let that affect what might be the last holiday he can ever afford. He is going to enjoy himself. May he come aboard, please?

Vince Of course.

Keith Thank you.

Vince But first, I would like your undertaking that you'll be prepared to accept the discipline of this craft as enforced by me, the skipper.

Keith No, I'm sorry, he's not accepting any provisions, he's coming aboard. I don't intend——

Vince Full ahead.

Fleur Full ahead, Skipper.

Keith What are you doing?

Emma Are we just leaving him behind?

June Bye.

Keith (*receding into the distance*) Right, it's the police this time. I'm fetching the police. This is your fault, Wingate, damn you.

Alistair Me?

Keith You just stood by, didn't you? You stood by. You spineless little rat. I'm suing you for everything. Everything you have . . .

Keith disappears from view

Vince Full ahead as she goes, helmsman.

Fleur Full ahead as she goes, Skipper.

June Silly little man——

Vince (*to June*) Get that weevil cleaned and then start on the dodger.

June Yes, Skipper.

Emma goes below. Alistair is still gazing aft towards Keith

Vince Lightning, you are idling about doing nothing, you are on half rations. Cookie?

Emma (*from the saloon*) Yes, Skipper?

Vince Please note that Lightning is on half rations until further notice.

Emma Tell him, looking at this curry, he's extremely lucky, Skipper.

Vince And you're for the towpath very shortly, Cookie.

Emma Ay, ay, Skipper.

Fleur Bridge.

The boat passes under a railway bridge. A train thunders above them. When they emerge from the shadow of the bridge, it is evening

Alistair is still sitting astern, cold, huddled and uncomfortable. June comes back on deck in an anorak. Emma comes up in her life-jacket and hat. Fleur still drives. Vince alone seems immune to the elements

Vince I make it we're now about twelve miles from Armageddon Bridge. Do it in one push tomorrow morning.

June Are we stopping soon? We've been going non-stop all day, Skipper.
Vince Have to keep up the schedule, Ginger.
June What's this ahead, Skipper? I've never been up this far.
Vince Pauper's Lock. Highest lock in the river.
June Porpoise as in fish?
Vince No, pauper as in victim of the system.
June Oh.
Emma Are we going to be able to shop tonight, Skipper?
Vince Not tonight, Cookie.
Emma We're practically out of everything.
Vince Improvise, Cookie, improvise.
Emma What with? (*She goes down into the saloon*)
Vince Take the port channel here, helmsman.
Fleur That's the weir, Skipper.
Vince Yes.
Fleur Starboard channel's the lock.
Vince I know what I'm doing, thank you, helmsman.
Fleur Sorry I spoke, Skipper.
Vince Stand by for mooring fore and aft.
June Oh, thank God. (*She clambers up forward*)
Vince All right back there, Lightning?
Alistair Yes, Skipper.
Vince Slow ahead.
Fleur Slow ahead, Skipper.
Vince Come in alongside that island. Nice little island.
Fleur We don't want to go much further. The current's quite strong. We're getting near the weir.
Vince This'll do here.
Fleur Not good mooring.
Vince Do as you're told.
Fleur Ay ay, Skipper.
Vince Stand by your scuffs. Make fast forward.

June jumps off with her bow rope

June Uh. It's disgustingly muddy.
Vince Make fast aft.

Alistair jumps off too

Alistair (*landing in more mud*) Oh, hell.
June Not a very good place to moor.
Vince Can you get back on again, Ginger. Just testing.
June Yes, OK. (*She climbs on*)

Alistair goes to follow her

Vince Not you, Lightning. Hang on there.
Alistair Oh, OK. (*He looks around him*) This is an island, isn't it?
Vince That's right. (*He moves up to the stern*)
June (*safely aboard*) Bow scuff aboard, Skipper.
Vince Hey, Lightning.

Alistair Hallo.

Vince Sling us your scuff, will you? Want to show you something.

Alistair Oh, right. Catch. (*He throws it*)

Vince (*retrieving it*) Ta. All right, full astern.

Fleur Full astern, Skipper.

Alistair Hey, what's happening?

Vince calmly coils up the rope

June Hey, wait a minute.

Vince (*to Fleur*) Bring us out into mid-stream and drop anchor.

Fleur I hope you've got a stern anchor. You'll need two in this current.

Alistair Hey, I say.

June Look, you've left Alistair.

Vince (*clambering forward*) This'll do. Stop engines.

Fleur Stop engines, Skipper. (*She does so, leaving the engine ticking over*)

Vince Excuse me, Ginger. (*He pushes past her*)

June You've left Alistair behind.

Vince Just get aft, Ginger, you're in the way. (*He heaves the mud anchor over the prow of the boat*) Let her drift back a bit.

Alistair Hi. Help. I say.

Fleur You're going to need a kedge to hold her.

Vince I'll see if we've got one. (*He moves aft*)

Emma (*coming up on deck*) What's happening?

Vince Slow ahead.

Fleur Slow ahead.

Vince (*finding a small anchor in the cockpit locker*) Here we are.

Emma What's that?

Fleur It's a kedge.

Emma He told us the kedge was a deck.

Fleur Who, Vince? I wouldn't believe anything he says. He wrecked Daddy's boat.

Vince (*throwing anchor over the stern*) Kedge's away. Switch off.

Fleur Switch off. (*She does so*)

Alistair I say, don't forget me, will you?

Emma (*seeing Alistair for the first time*) What's Alistair doing there?

Alistair Hallo. I seem to be marooned.

Emma Vince. What is Alistair doing there?

Alistair Hallo.

Vince (*calling*) Lightning.

Alistair Yes.

Vince It was the opinion of the majority of the crew, Lightning, that you were getting a bit soft. A bit flabby, you see.

Alistair Oh yes.

Vince So we thought you could do with a little toughening up. Touch of the Duke of Edinburgh Awards, all right?

Alistair Oh. Well.

Emma Just a minute. What do you mean, we? Who's we? We thought this, we thought that.

Vince Somebody saying something.

Emma Skipper.

Vince Cookie?

Emma What is my husband doing marooned on an island?

Vince We're toughening him up for you, Cookie.

Emma Well, thank you very much but I don't happen to want him toughened up . . .

As Vince moves away

Skipper, I married him soft and I married him flabby and I like him that way. And if you leave him on that island all night in this temperature, he will die of pneumonia. Now get him back aboard, please. Skipper. Please . . .

Vince Request denied, Cookie. Start the supper.

Emma I'm not starting anything, Skipper, until my husband's here.

Vince The sooner you cook something, the sooner he's back aboard. Suit yourself. Now pay attention. Can you hear me, Lightning?

Alistair Yes.

Vince Tomorrow will be our last day heading upstream. We've only a few miles to go till we reach Armageddon Bridge. After that, we'll be returning downstream. Now this entails turning the whole boat the other way round. Therefore what is now our port side will become our starboard and what is now our stern will become our bow. Now that is going to take a bit of getting used to. You'll all need practice. So as from tomorrow, that — (*pointing left*) — becomes starboard and that — (*pointing right*) — becomes port side. Similarly, forward — (*pointing aft*) and aft — (*pointing forward*). All right, carry on. (*He goes into the saloon*)

Emma (*in a whisper*) He's mad. He's totally mad.

June It sounds quite logical to me. (*She goes down after Vince*)

Emma We're on a boat with a madman.

Fleur I wouldn't shout too loud, Cookie. We might be needing a third anchor. (*She goes into the saloon*)

Emma I'm on a boat with a madman. (*Calling*) Alistair.

Alistair Hallo.

Emma What are you going to do?

Alistair Sit here and wait for rescue, I suppose.

Emma You can't stay there.

Alistair Not much choice.

Emma You can swim.

Alistair Not in this. It's quite fierce. We're very near the weir. Dangerous.

Emma Alistair, will you not be so bloody calm about it. You've just been turned off the boat you've paid for with the holiday money we saved and you've been marooned on a deserted island with no food or drink or shelter. And you're just sitting there. He's right. You're flabby.

Alistair Look, I'm not going to get anywhere by screaming with rage and bashing my head against the bullrushes, am I? I might as well make the best of it.

Emma (*wearily*) OK.

From below, the chant of "Food, food, food" from Vince, Fleur and June

I'd better start cooking. (*She goes down into the saloon*)

Alistair sits on the island as it grows dark. The saloon and forward cabin lights come on. Keith's voice is heard distantly

Keith (*off; distant*) Wingate. Alistair Wingate.
Alistair Hallo?
Keith (*off*) Keith Taylor is going to hound you, Wingate. He's going to hound you for the rest of your life.
Alistair Oh, Lord.

June and Fleur come out of the saloon, followed by Vince. They cross to the aft cabin. June and Fleur go in. The aft cabin lights come on

Vince Good-night, Lightning. (*He opens the cockpit locker and brings out a fresh coil of rope. As he goes down the aft steps*) Right. Knotcraft time.
June (*from within, laughing a little apprehensively*) Oh, now, Vince, Vince.

Vince closes the aft doors. The odd thump, bump and squeak from June and occasional laugh from Vince or Fleur. The saloon and forward cabin lights go off. In a moment, Emma comes on deck. She is in her dressing-gown and wearing her life-jacket over the top. She carries a plastic carrier bag

Emma (*whispering*) Alistair. Alistair.
Alistair Emma.
Emma I got you a tin of beans and a tin of creamed rice.
Alistair Ah.
Emma I've had to open them though.
Alistair Open them?
Emma In case they miss the opener. I've wrapped them in clingfilm so they shouldn't spill. But I can't throw them. I'm going to rig a breeches-buoy.
Alistair A what?

Emma looks in the cockpit locker

Emma Damn. Someone's taken all the rope. Hang on.
June (*muffled from the aft cabin*) I'm Gingernut June, hallo. Tippy-tapping a tune, doopy-doopy doo ... oooh. (*The last, a cry of pain*)
Emma What are they doing? What are they doing?
Alistair Don't worry.
Vince ⎫
Fleur ⎬ (*in muffled chorus*)
June ⎭   Introducing those Gingernuts
     Three fresh baked Gingernuts
     Three kids who badly want to sing you
     Numbers that will bring you
     Memories ... (*The song ends in laughter*)

During this Emma fetches the bow rope which is unused, of course, since they are at anchor. She unhitches the rope from its fixing and brings it to the cockpit

Emma Coming over.

Emma throws the line. It carries near enough for Alistair to grab it

Alistair Well thrown. Bravo. Now what?
Emma It's going to have to be longer. It's got to return. Hang on. Ssh.

Emma creeps astern over the heads of the carousers in the aft cabin. Carefully she unfastens the stern line and returns

Here. Catch hold of this ...

Emma hurls the entire rope to Alistair

Alistair Got it.
Emma Now tie it to the other one, then throw me the loose end.
Alistair OK. You're a brilliant woman.
Emma Get on with it. God help us if they catch us.

Another burst of laughter from the aft cabin. Emma peers through the cabin doors. During the next, Emma ties the shopping bag near to the end of the bow rope. Alistair, meanwhile, gropes around in the dark, finds two ends of rope and ties them together. In fact, mistakenly, he ties together both ends of the stern rope

Alistair, they're all in bed together.
Alistair Yes, I saw.
Emma They wanted me as well.
Alistair What did you say?
Emma I said I wanted to wash up. Alistair, I'm very frightened. What's happening? What's happening?
Alistair I think it's called the final collapse of civilization as we know it.
Emma Right. Now carefully, find your loose end and throw it back to me.
Alistair Brilliant. She's a brilliant woman. Do you wear that all the time now? Your life-jacket?
Emma Oh, yes. I've started sleeping in it.
Alistair Oh.
Emma Come on.
Alistair (*having completed his task*) OK. Right. (*He fumbles around and finds the end of the original bow rope. He picks it up and in so doing threads it through the circle he has made with the stern rope*)
Emma Ready.
Alistair Here it comes.

Alistair hurls the bow rope back. Emma catches it

All right?
Emma Got it. Wait a second. I'll complete the circle.

Emma now ties the end of the bow rope she's received from Alistair to the other end of the bow rope with the shopping bag

Right. We'll take it clockwise. All right? Just gently.
Alistair Brilliant.

Alistair stands inside his stern rope loop and pulls taut against Emma's bow rope loop which she is standing inside. They carefully pay out their respective loops but, of course, when the bag gets halfway it jams. Emma tugs in vain. Alistair, meeting no such obstruction, continues happily revolving his stern rope

Emma What's happened?
Alistair What?
Emma It's stopped.
Alistair No, it hasn't.
Emma It's stuck.
Alistair My bit's still moving.
Emma It can't be. Your bit can't be moving unless my bit's moving. Alistair, what have you done? What are you doing?
Alistair I haven't done anything. My bit's moving. It's your bit.
Emma (*losing all restraint*) Alistair, you're useless. What's the point of trying to help someone who's quite so weedy and useless?
Alistair I don't see why you pick on——(*He breaks off*)

Vince has appeared behind Emma. Fleur also comes up and stands in the doorway. Vince smiles at Emma

Emma (*swallowing*) Oh, I'm . . . I'm . . .
Vince Well, well. Somebody else having fun with rope, are they? Can I help at all? (*He reveals his other hand to be holding his knife*)
Emma We were just . . . I was just . . .

Vince makes a sudden movement which causes Emma to release the rope. The shopping basket drops into the water

Oh.
Vince There you go.
Emma Thank you.
Vince I think we're going to have to deal with you in the morning.
Emma Now, look, you're not—you're not frightening me. Not. Not.
Vince We'll have to think of something for you in the morning, won't we?
Fleur I'll tell you what.
Vince What?
Fleur We could make her walk the plank. That'd be great fun. Help to teach her to swim.
Vince True. Corrective and instructive. That's what I like.
Fleur It happens on all the best pirate ships.
Vince The plank it shall be.
Emma I'm not—I'm certainly not planking. I'm sorry. No, sorry.
June (*from the aft cabin*) I say, where's everyone gone?
Vince (*to Emma*) You'd better get some sleep.
Emma No, I'm sorry. Not a plank.
Vince Off you go. Night-night.

Vince opens the aft hatch to allow Emma to look down into the cabin

June (*from the aft cabin*) Where are you all? This is most terribly uncomfortable. Please.

Whatever Emma sees, causes her to scream and scuttle down into the saloon, slamming the doors behind her. Fleur laughs delightedly and makes to chase her, finally going back to the aft cabin. Vince follows her

Vince (*as he goes*) Night-night, Lightning. Enjoy your supper, won't you? (*He closes the aft cabin doors*)

Alistair fishes the ropes and sodden polythene bag out of the water. He looks inside. He produces the tin of beans but they are obviously now inedible. He lays them all aside with a sigh. Emma's head pops up through the forward hatch

Emma Alistair?
Alistair Hallo.
Emma What am I going to do?
Alistair It's OK, don't worry. I'm OK.
Emma What about me? I've got to walk the plank in the morning.
Alistair It'll be OK. Don't worry. Try and sleep.
Emma How can I sleep? Didn't you hear him? They're going to make me walk the plank.
Alistair (*shrugging*) Well.
Emma Oh, God. (*She is about to close the hatch*)
Alistair Emma?
Emma Yes.
Alistair If it's any consolation ...
Emma What?
Alistair I don't think they've got a plank on board.
Emma (*only a little consoled*) Oh. (*She closes her hatch*)

Alistair sits unhappily. Eventually the aft cabin lights go off. Time passes. Dawn arrives. A clap of thunder. With it, comes the rain. It is this that awakens Alistair who is curled up in a bundle

Alistair Wha? Ah. (*He crouches for rudimentary shelter*)

Vince comes on deck. He has his captain's hat on. He has made no concessions to the weather in the rest of his clothing. He carries the cassette radio and a few cassettes

Vince Ah, good-morning, Lightning.
Alistair Good-morning.
Vince Sleep well? I trust you did. We'll be along to pick you up in a minute. If you'd care to come aboard. (*Indicating the radio*) Thought I'd borrow this to check the weather forecast. If you don't mind it getting rained on. (*He puts it by the wheel. Shouting behind him*) Come on, you lot. Time we were underway. I want to be at Armageddon by noon.

Fleur comes up the steps of the aft cabin. She is putting the final stitch in a home-made pirate flag she has been making. A standard black base with a skull and crossbones in white

Fleur Sometimes you're too hearty for your own good, Skipper.
Vince What've you got there, first mate?
Fleur (*holding up her flag*) Har-har ...

Vince Har. 'Tis the jolliest of Rogers I have ever seen. Sling it from the yardarm.

Fleur Ay ay, Skipper. (*She goes to the stern and unties the standard hire-boat Red Ensign that hangs there. Tossing this to one side (but not in the water) she ties her own flag there instead*)

Meanwhile, June lurches on to the deck. She is very feeble indeed. Incongruously, she is dressed in a version of her Gingernut gear. Her vivid make-up is streaked and ghastly in the morning light

June Oh.

Vince Come on, Ginger.

June Oh. I think I've done something awful to my back.

Vince On the bow anchor if you please. (*He starts the engine*)

June (*hurrying to do so*) Yes, Skipper.

Vince Haul away on the stern anchor, me boys.

Fleur Ay ay, Skipper. (*She pulls the smaller stern anchor aboard*)

Vince Haul away on the forward anchor, Ginger.

June Ay ay. (*Tugging*) Oh. I'm sorry, I can't.

Vince Come on.

June I'm sorry. It's my back, you see.

Vince Half rations for Ginger.

Fleur Half rations for Ginger.

June It's no good, Vince. I'm a woman. Women aren't supposed to haul anchors.

Vince Quarter rations for Ginger.

Fleur Quarter rations for Ginger.

Vince Give her a hand.

Fleur Ay ay, Skipper.

June It's a man's job, hauling in anchors.

Vince Where's our Cookie this morning? Come on, Cookie. Wakey wakey. (*He thumps on the saloon doors*)

Fleur hauls in the bow anchor with some ease

June I'm going to put something on. I'm getting soaked out here. (*She goes back to the aft cabin*)

Fleur Bow anchors away, Skipper.

Vince All right, Lightning, we're coming for you.

Vince starts to manoeuvre the craft to the bank, where Alistair waits

June comes out of the aft cabin holding the remains of a black slip. It has an enormous hole cut out of it with what look like nail scissors

June I've just found this on the floor. Who's responsible for this? Who did this to my slip?

Fleur Yours, was it?

June Of course it was mine. Did you do this?

Fleur Yes.

June Well, you destructive little ... Why, why?

Fleur (*indicating the flag*) For the good of the ship.

June (*surveying the flag*) You did that with my slip? You made a flag out of my silk slip?

Fleur You should see what I made the skull and crossbones out of.

June That is spiteful. That really is. That's just spiteful.

Vince Now, now, that's enough, Ginger. (*He switches off the engine*)

June Have you seen what she's done?

Vince (*dangerously*) That is enough.

June Yes, but have you seen——

Vince (*in a terrible voice*) Yes, Skipper. When you talk to me, you will say yes, Skipper or no, Skipper. Do you understand that?

June (*quite frightened*) Yes, Skipper.

Vince Have you got that through your thick head, you stupid, ugly middle-aged ginger tart? Have you?

June (*in a tiny voice*) Yes, Skipper.

Vince (*quieter*) Good. Because I am not saying it again. Not ever again. (*Shouting*) I'm going to have discipline aboard my boat. (*To Alistair*) You. Come aboard.

Alistair Yes, righty-ho, Skipper.

Vince And perhaps you'd be so good as to bring the remains of my mooring ropes aboard with you when you come.

Alistair Righty-ho. Skipper. (*He goes to retrieve them*)

Fleur Want me to make fast?

Vince No, we're OK here. We're on the mud, we won't drift. (*Brightening up*) Come on, then, where's Cookie? Where's our Cookie hiding this morning? (*Looking through the saloon doors*) Ah, here she is. Come up on deck then.

Emma comes up from the saloon very reluctantly. She is fully dressed and has on her life-jacket

Good-morning.

Emma (*bravely*) Good-morning, Skipper.

Vince Well now, I think it's about plank-walking time, don't you?

Emma I think this whole thing's very silly and getting out of hand. And I wish to say——

Fleur Only one snag, we haven't got a plank.

Emma No, you haven't got a plank, have you?

Vince Haven't got a plank? What do you mean, we haven't got a plank? (*He marches forward and disappears into the cabin*)

Alistair meanwhile is climbing aboard, with the ropes

Alistair (*to Emma*) Hallo.

Emma Hallo.

Alistair Rotten morning.

Emma Yes.

Alistair You mustn't worry. He's only ... He won't——

A roar from Vince in the forward cabin and the terrible sound of splintering wood

June Oh dear God, what's he doing?

Vince returns on deck. Under his arm, what must have been a locker door, ripped off at its hinges

June That's their bedroom door.
Vince Now it's a plank.
June This is a rented boat, you know. You really can't ... (*She tails off feebly*)
Vince Mind your backs.

He goes to the bow and wedges the plank on the deck between the stanchions and the deck. It sticks out over the water

Fleur You won't need your life-jacket on.
Emma Oh yes I will, I can't swim.
Fleur You can't walk the plank in a life-jacket, come on.
Emma You try. Just you try. (*She backs away determinedly*)
Vince Let her keep it on.
Fleur It's stupid.
Vince If she floats a bit, she can show us the speed of the current. (*Testing the plank*) That seems to be OK. (*To Emma*) Over here, then.
June She'll be all right, will she? I mean, you're not going to ...

Emma moves reluctantly to the foot of the plank

Vince All right then. Off you go.
Fleur Just a second. (*She snatches the piece of slip from June's hands and moves to Emma*) Must do it properly. Keep still. (*She blindfolds Emma with the silk*) That's more like it.
Vince All right, then. Away you go.

Emma hesitates

Come on.
Fleur Come on, then.
Emma (*quietly, trying to subdue her panic*) Alistair ... Alistair ...
Alistair You'll be OK, Emma. You'll be fine.
Vince Come on. You want me to give you a hand or something.
Emma (*taking a second step*) Alistair ...
Vince And another. Long way to go yet.
Fleur Come on.
June You won't really let her ...

Emma takes a third step

I mean, she'll fall in.
Emma Alistair, please help me.
Alistair Er—it's ... it's a bit ...
Vince Come on, and again.

Emma takes a fourth step

Alistair It's OK, Emma ...

Emma Alistair, it is not OK. In another fifteen seconds, I'm going to step off
a plank into a river.
Fleur And again.
Vince Again.

Emma takes a fifth step

Alistair (*in an agony of indecision*) Yes, well, I . . . oh, hell.

Emma takes a sixth step

Vince That's it.
Emma Alistair. In another five seconds, I am going to drown. I am going to
die. (*She is very near the edge now*)
Fleur (*maliciously*) Three or four steps yet. You've plenty to go.
Emma (*her control going in a great scream*) Alistair, help me. Please, Alistair,
help me.
Vince One more step.

Alistair makes a decision

Alistair All right — er — all right. Stop that. I'm afraid you're going to have to
stop this, please. Sorry. Stop it.
Vince You'd better keep clear of this, Lightning, or you'll go back on your
island.
Alistair (*pushing past them with mounting anger*) I said, stop it and I mean,
stop it. Now, stop it, you stupid, stupid senseless people. That is my wife.
On this plank. My wife. Whom I love. So get away. (*He seizes Emma, pulls
her off the plank and tugs away her blindfold*)
Emma Oh.
Vince (*after a pause*) OK, Lightning. Now, let's see you do the plank instead,
shall we?
Alistair No. Enough's enough. We're getting off now.
Vince Getting off?
Alistair Yes. You can have the boat. Have all our things. I don't care. We'd
just like to get home.
Vince I don't think you've quite grasped the rules of the sea, Lightning.
Nobody leaves their ship without the skipper's permission. That's known
as shore leave. You're not due for that for about four years.
Alistair Well, I'm sorry. You'd better take that up with the Admiralty. We're
getting off.
Vince The only way you'll get off this boat is by getting past me, Lightning.
Would you care to try?
Alistair Yes.
Vince What?
Alistair I'd care to try, yes.
Emma (*in a awed whisper*) Alistair.
June Oh, no . . .
Fleur He'll kill you.
Vince All right. Would it be best if we stepped ashore?
Alistair Just as you like.

Vince (*to Fleur, indicating the plank*) Put that away for later, will you?
Fleur Ay ay, Skipper.

Vince climbs ashore to the island and waits for Alistair. Fleur dismantles the plank and lays it on the deck

Alistair June?
June (*rather blank*) Yes.
Alistair Would you look after Emma, please?
June You're not going to fight him, are you, Alistair?
Alistair Yes, I think that's the idea.
Fleur I should warn you he's been in twice for GBH.
Alistair Committed whilst in his bird sanctuary, was it?
Fleur What?
Vince Come on then, Lightning.
Emma Oh, Alistair.
Alistair Won't be a moment.

Alistair climbs ashore to face Vince. Fleur follows and finds a good vantage point from which to watch the action. June and Emma stay further removed. Emma still, in fact, recovering from her ordeal

Vince (*genially*) I'm going to do you a favour, Lightning. When I fight which I have been known to do quite a lot of in my time, I don't usually tell people in advance what I'm going to do to them. I like to make it a surprise. But in your case, I'll be friendly. So. Number one. I'm going to break your nose, all right?
Alistair Yes.
Vince And I should think about three ribs.
Alistair Fine, yes.
Vince And you're going to lose about four of your front teeth.
Alistair Right.
Vince I'm going to smash one arm and make sure you limp for the rest of your life. OK?
Alistair Yes, right. That sounds very reasonable. Well.

Alistair swings a sudden swift blow at Vince, hoping to catch him unawares. Vince parries it with his forearm

Vince Ow.

He raises a hand to Alistair's face. Alistair instinctively brings up an arm to protect himself. Vince slams in the most awful body punch that sends Alistair down like a lead sack.

Alistair Huh.

Emma vibrates from the blow as well. The fight starts. Alistair doing little or no damage to Vince. He finds by holding on tightly he can avoid some of the more savage and swinging blows. All the same, he takes an awful hammering. The men slither down the bank into the shallow water. A mostly silent affair. The women, too, speak softly

Emma (*during this*) Oh Alistair. Dear, dear Alistair.
June Oh. (*Averting her gaze*) Oh, this is appalling.
Fleur Go on, Vince. Get him, Vince. Kill him, Vince.
Emma Oh, please, please don't do any more to him.
June Somebody ought to stop this. Somebody should stop it.

The fight ends with Vince sitting half in the water. He has hold of the back of Alistair's hair

Vince (*breathless*) Now. Let's see how much river you can drink, Lightning.

Vince is about to plunge Alistair's face into the water

Fleur (*suddenly, urgently, softly*) Vince! ... Vince!
Vince (*stopping, startled*) What?
Fleur (*low and urgent*) Don't move, Vince, whatever you do. Just hold it. Don't move.
Vince What—? (*He lets go of Alistair and turns to her*) What is it?
Fleur (*pointing*) Look.

Alistair brings his hand out of the water. It is holding the baked bean tin. He looks at it. He looks at Vince who is turned away from him

Vince Where?
Fleur (*in a low, excited voice*) It's the kingfisher, Vince. It's the kingfisher.

Alistair brings the bean tin down on Vince's head

Vince I'll give you bloody kingfi——(*The blow lands*) Shit. (*Turning back to Alistair*) Now, that is going to cost you ...

Alistair repeats the blow

    You sly little ... Lightning. (*He crashes down into the water*)
Fleur (*whose bird has flown*) Oh, now, look what you've done—you——(*She sees Vince*)
June Vince. Oh, God. He's killed Vince. You've killed Vince.
Fleur What's happened?

June rushes to Vince. So does Fleur. They pull him from the water and lay him on the bank. His head is bleeding. Alistair, meanwhile, is crawling and staggering to the boat

Fleur My God, look what he's done to Vince. What have you done to Vince, you bastard?
Emma (*coming to meet Alistair at the edge of the boat*) Alistair ...
Alistair (*in a terrible state*) Hallo, back again.
Emma (*helping him aboard*) Oh, Alistair. Alistair, Alistair, Alistair, Alistair, Alistair ...
Alistair I think I need ... I think I need a bit of a lie down.
Emma (*guiding him to the aft cabin*) Yes, you lie down. I'll get the first aid.

Emma steers him into the aft cabin and returns immediately and rushes into the saloon

June (*meantime*) He hit him with a tin. I think it was a tin.

Fleur It's quite deep. He'll need stitches. Little bastard. I'll find a first-aid kit. Have you got any first aid?

June There's some in the mizen.

Fleur In the where?

June In the saloon.

Fleur goes to climb aboard. Emma by now is returning from the saloon with her large first-aid tin. She also carries a carving knife in her other hand

Emma (*seeing Fleur*) Oh no, you don't. You keep off this boat.

Fleur What?

Emma Get off. I warn you. I'll cut you if you do. (*Brandishing the knife*) I will. I'll cut——

Fleur (*backing off*) Look, all I want is some first aid.

Emma You find your own first aid.

Fleur Look, you can't deny this man first aid. He's bleeding badly.

Emma Good. (*Relenting, putting the knife between her teeth*) Here. There's a bandage. (*She hurls it at Fleur*) And some lint. (*She throws that*) And that's a tube of something. (*She throws that*) And that's all you're getting. Now, go away.

Fleur grubs along the bank for the items Emma has thrown. June cradles Vince who is beginning to recover consciousness. Emma goes into the aft cabin, gets rid of the first-aid tin and returns almost immediately

June He's coming round.

Emma (*calling back into the aft cabin*) Won't be a second, love.

She starts the engine

Fleur (*looking up, startled*) Hoy.

Emma puts the boat into forward gear and moves away to mid-river

June What are you doing? Come back. We've got a sick man here.

Vince (*coming up on his knees, weakly*) You bring my boat back here, do you hear? You bring my boat back.

June Come back.

Fleur Come back.

They go out of earshot

Emma (*calling behind her*) Alistair.

Alistair (*from below aft, weakly*) Hallo.

Emma Upstream or downstream?

Alistair I don't know.

Emma Come on, you're the skipper, up or down?

Alistair Up. Upstream, of course.

Emma Right. Full ahead, then.

Alistair Full ahead.

Emma begins to relax. They pass under a bridge. Time passes. She reaches for the cassette radio. She turns it on. A very faint voice can be heard

(*From below*) What are you doing up there? What are you listening to?

Emma Sorry, was it disturbing you? I was just trying to hear Woman's Hour. The reception's not very good. You've been asleep for hours.

Alistair Must have been.

Emma Would you like some music?

Alistair Sure.

Emma (*examining the cassettes*) James Last.

Alistair No, thanks.

Emma Verdi's Requiem.

Alistair Not at the moment.

Emma Brahms, Debussy, Bach.

Alistair No. Something English. We need something English, damn it.

Emma William Byrd.

Alistair Splendid. Just the chap.

Emma starts the cassette: "The Earl of Oxford's March" rings out across the river. It rings out at a volume far greater than any cassette machine could ever give it. As it plays, Alistair slowly comes up the aft steps. Emma turns and smiles at her new hero. Alistair is very bruised, one arm is in a sling. Keith's blazer is over his shoulder giving him the appearance of having one arm. One eye is covered with a black patch. Emma hands him the captain's hat. Alistair puts it on. He extends his good hand to Emma. They stand for a moment. He takes the wheel. Emma goes aft and unties the pirate flag from the stern flagpole. She replaces it with the Red Ensign. Alistair throttles back the engine and turns off the music

Emma What is it?

Alistair Look. (*He points ahead*)

An awed silence

Emma It's the bridge.

Alistair Armageddon Bridge.

Emma Armageddon Bridge.

Alistair It gets very narrow here.

Emma Yes.

Alistair Hard to turn round.

Emma If they're waiting for us here, we've had it. Sitting ducks.

Alistair Yes.

Emma Go very carefully.

Alistair I will.

Emma Dead slow ahead.

Alistair Dead slow ahead, Skipper. Keep your eyes peeled.

They both anxiously scan the banks ahead of them. The silence is eerie

   Suddenly, Vince is on the bank behind them. A bedraggled sight in a bloodstained bandage

Vince Lightning.

Emma and Alistair turn

   I want my boat, Lightning. I want my boat back. You've reached the end of the road, Lightning. You've got to come back this way now. We've got a little matter to settle, haven't we?

Fleur appears beside him

Fleur (*overlapping*) We'll be waiting for you, Cookie. You can't go under that bridge. You've got to come back. We've got the plank ready for you.

June joins them

June (*overlapping*) We're all waiting for you, Alistair. We've got you now. You can't escape. Tell him, Emma. Tell him he can't escape.

Mrs Hatfield appears

Mrs Hatfield (*adding her voice to theirs*) Got you now, Alistair Wingate. You're trapped. Trapped like the little capitalist rat you are. We're going to put you in a cage where you belong.

Keith appears

Keith (*overlapping*) You're not allowed under that bridge, Alistair. You've got to stop and turn round. It's one of the conditions of hire. And once you've turned round, Keith Taylor will be waiting for you, you traitor. Keith Taylor will hound you, Wingate. He will hound you.

All their voices are now shouting at once. Alistair and Emma remain fascinated by this scene behind them. They're so riveted by their pursuers, they fail to see where they're going

Emma (*looking ahead*) Alistair! Alistair, look out, we're going under the bridge.

Suddenly all the voices behind them become distorted and booming. It grows very dark

The sounds of the pursuers fade as they exit

Although Emma speaks low, her voice is loud and booming

Oh my God, we're going under Armageddon Bridge.
Alistair It's OK. We'll be OK.

A sudden grinding crash as the boat runs aground. The engine stops. Silence

Emma (*from the darkness*) Alistair?

During the Black-out, Emma and Alistair go below to the aft cabin. Suddenly it's the morning of the seventh day. Bright sunshine. Birdsong. The boat has indeed run aground and sits at a slight angle

Alistair comes up from the aft cabin. He has lost his eye-patch and his sling but is still quite stiff and bruised. He wears his captain's hat. He stands on the deck and surveys the scene. In a moment, Emma joins him, still in her life-jacket

Where are we now?
Alistair Just the far side of Armageddon Bridge, I think. We seem to have discovered the absolute limit of navigation.

Emma (*smiling*) Yes. It's so beautiful.
Alistair Yes.
Emma Peaceful.
Alistair Yes.
Emma Shall we stay here? For ever? They'd never find us. Not this far upstream. Nobody ever comes this far upstream.
Alistair No. We'll have to go back.
Emma Why? There's nothing there now. No job, no friends. Nothing. Not anymore. Just enemies. People who hate us.
Alistair We still have to go back.
Emma But they're all so — unreasonable.
Alistair Then we reasonable people will just have to go back and reason with them.
Emma Oh, well. If that's what you want.
Alistair You agree though?
Emma Oh, yes. It's just so beautiful here.
Alistair Well, we can have a holiday. No harm in that.
Emma For a few days.
Alistair Yes.
Emma All right. What would you like to do for your holiday?
Alistair Er — I don't know.
Emma I'll tell you what. Let's both take off our clothes and jump over the side of the boat and swim to that island over there and maybe we could lie together in the sun for a little and . . . then we'd——
Alistair Make love . . .
Emma Yes. Well . . .
Alistair Sounds fine.

Emma discards her life-jacket. They both start to undress. Alistair stares at her

Emma (*a little embarrassed*) What's the matter?
Alistair I'd forgotten how lovely you were without your life-jacket.
Emma Oh.
Alistair All right?

He takes her hand and they move to the side of the boat

Emma (*a little nervously*) Yes, I think so.
Alistair Don't be frightened.
Emma No. If I sink, you could always lifesave me, couldn't you? Do you know how to do that? I lie flat on my back, you see, and you lie on your back beneath me . . . (*smiling*) . . . and you slip your arm under my arm and . . . so on and so on and so on . . .
Alistair (*smiling too*) I see. I see. Ready?
Emma Ready.

They remove the rest of their clothes

Alistair And one, two, three — jump.

As they make to jump into the water a swift——

BLACK-OUT

FURNITURE AND PROPERTY LIST

ACT I

On stage: River bank with mooring points, grass, pebbles etc.
Boat — see text page 1 for description
On forward deck: bow rope and fixing (moored to bank at start), mud anchor and rope, boat hook, hatch (practical)
On aft deck: aft rope and fixing (moored to bank at start), stern flagpole with Red Ensign flag, hatch (practical)
In cockpit; wheel, hooter (practical), locker containing 2 mooring irons, mallet, 2 coils of rope, small anchor

Off stage: Torch (practical), luggage, life-jackets (**Keith**)
Luggage (**June**)
Luggage, box of groceries, first-aid box containing bandages, lint, cream, portable cassette radio (**Emma**)
Torch (practical), luggage (**Alistair**)

The following properties are required on the boat during Act I and should be set as follows:

In aft cabin: Book: *River Cruising on the Orb*, map (**Keith**)
Rug, beach bag (**June**)
In saloon: Bacon sandwich (**Alistair**)
2 mugs coffee (**Emma**)
Bacon sandwich (**Emma**)
Cigarettes, matches (**Alistair**)
Mop, bucket (**Alistair**)

Personal: **Vince:** pendant on gold chain, knife in belt
Keith: money in pocket

ACT II

Off stage: Cardboard crate containing bottles of wine (**Vince**)
Bag containing bottles, roll of belongings (**Fleur**)
Binoculars (**Fleur**)

The following properties are required on the boat during Act II and should be set as follows

In aft cabin: Purse containing money (**June**)
Briefcase, toilet items (**Keith**)
Pirate flag, needle and thread (**Fleur**)
Black slip with ragged hole (**June**)
Cassette radio, cassettes, concealed blood sac (**Vince**)
Sling, black eye-patch, Keith's blazer (**Alistair**)
In saloon: Duster (**June**)

Mop, bucket **(Keith)**
Washing-up bowl of water **(Alistair)**
Glass of wine **(Fleur)**
Glass of wine **(Emma)**
Glass of wine **(June)**
Bottle of wine **(Vince)**
Plastic carrier bag containing opened tins of beans, creamed rice **(Emma)**
First-aid kit containing bandages, lint, cream; carving knife **(Emma)**
In forward cabin: "Plank" **(Vince)**

Personal: **Vince:** bloodstained bandage (for page 84)

LIGHTING PLOT

Practical fittings required: Lights in forward cabin, saloon/galley, aft cabin, cockpit
Exterior: a boat and surrounding river and banks

ACT I

To open: Moonlight effect

Cue 1	**Keith** goes below to switch on lights. *Snap on forward cabin, saloon/galley lights*	(Page 3)
Cue 2	**Keith** moves into aft cabin to switch on lights *Snap on aft cabin lights*	(Page 3)
Cue 3	**Keith** switches on cockpit lights *Snap on cockpit light and covering spots*	(Page 3)
Cue 4	**Keith** switches off cockpit lights *Snap off cockpit lights and covering spots*	(Page 8)
Cue 5	**Alistair** disappears below hatch to switch off lights *Pause, then snap off saloon and forward cabin lights; pause, then snap off aft cabin lights; gradually increase moonlight effect*	(Page 9)
Cue 6	**Keith:** "... shut up and go to sleep." *Snap on forward cabin lights*	(Page 9)
Cue 7	**Alistair** slams shut forward hatch; **June** stops crying *Snap off forward cabin lights*	(Page 10)
Cue 8	**Keith** (*muffled*): "... go to sleep." *Pause, then gradually bring up dawn effect, then general sunny daylight effect*	(Page 10)
Cue 9	**Keith:** "Bridge coming up." *Shadow effect as they pass under bridge*	(Page 13)
Cue 10	**Alistair:** "Ah." *Return to previous lighting level*	(Page 13)
Cue 11	**Emma:** "Ay ay, sir." (*She goes below*) *Gradually fade to sunset effect*	(Page 22)
Cue 12	**Keith** (*muffled*): "Oh, Jesus." *Snap on forward cabin lights*	(Page 22)
Cue 13	**Keith** (*muffled*): "Shut up." *Snap off forward cabin lights*	(Page 22)
Cue 14	**Alistair** and **Emma** go below *Pause, then bring up dawn effect, then general sunny daylight effect*	(Page 25)
Cue 15	**June** (*screaming*): "LOOK OUT!" *Shadow effect as steamer passes boat*	(Page 29)

Cue 16	**Alistair** follows **Emma** down into saloon *Gradually fade to dusk effect; snap on saloon lights*	(Page 37)
Cue 17	**Vince** goes below to saloon *Fade to Black-out*	(Page 38)

ACT II

To open: Bright sunshine effect

Cue 18	**June** and **Emma** go below *Gradually fade lights as darkness falls; snap on saloon lights*	(Page 56)
Cue 19	**June** hurries into her cabin *Snap on aft cabin lights*	(Page 59)
Cue 20	**Emma** follows **Alistair** below *Snap on forward cabin lights*	(Page 63)
Cue 21	**Fleur** moves forward away from sounds *Snap off forward cabin lights; pause, then snap off aft cabin lights*	(Page 64)
Cue 22	**Fleur** wanders off slowly into the darkness *Gradually bring up grey dawn effect, then grey daylight effect*	(Page 66)
Cue 23	**Fleur:** "Bridge." *Shadow effect as they pass under bridge; fade lights to early evening effect*	(Page 69)
Cue 24	**Emma** goes down into saloon; **Alistair** sits on island *Gradually fade lights as darkness falls; snap on saloon and forward cabin lights*	(Page 73)
Cue 25	**June** and **Fleur** go into aft cabin *Snap on aft cabin lights*	(Page 73)
Cue 26	**Vince** goes into aft cabin *Pause, then snap off saloon and forward cabin lights*	(Page 73)
Cue 27	**Emma** closes hatch; **Alistair** sits unhappily *Snap off aft cabin lights; pause, then gradually bring up grey dawn effect, gradually increasing to general dull daylight effect*	(Page 76)
Cue 28	**Alistair:** "Full ahead." *Pause, then shadow effect as they pass under bridge*	(Page 83)
Cue 29	**Emma:** ". . . under the bridge." *Shadow effect gradually dimming to Black-out*	(Page 85)
Cue 30	When ready *Bright sunshine effect*	(Page 85)
Cue 31	**Alistair:** ". . . two, three—jump." *Swift Black-out*	(Page 86)

EFFECTS PLOT

Cue 1   As CURTAIN rises   (Page 1)
Lapping water, splash of a water creature, cry of a nightbird

Cue 2   **Emma** goes below   (Page 7)
Splash of a water-vole

Cue 3   **Keith** goes below   (Page 8)
Clumping and bumping from both ends

Cue 4   **June** (*muffled*): "... even from you."   (Page 9)
Clumps and bangs aft

Cue 5   **Alistair** (*muffled*): "... bring it through."   (Page 9)
Loud bump forward

Cue 6   **June** (*muffled*): "Exactly."   (Page 9)
Clumps fore and aft

Cue 7   Forward cabin lights go out   (Page 9)
*Clumps aft; pause, then gentle lapping water, occasional nightbird
and animal sounds*

Cue 8   As dawn comes up   (Page 10)
Bird, water sounds, distant chug of other craft

Cue 9   **Keith:** "Come on, my beauty."   (Page 10)
One false start, then diesel engine starts

Cue 10   **Keith:** "And away we go."   (Page 11)
Engine slow ahead

Cue 11   **Alistair** (*not really hearing him*): "Yes?" (Page 11)
Engine full ahead

Cue 12   **June** settles down on deck   (Page 12)
Two hoots from passing craft

Cue 13   **Emma** goes below   (Page 14)
Pause, then music: Bach

Cue 14   **Alistair** goes below into saloon   (Page 15)
Pause, then stop music

Cue 15   **Keith** (*chuckling*): "... division of labour." (Page 15)
Horn hoot

Cue 16   **Keith:** "... as she's told."   (Page 16)
Engine throttles back

Cue 17   **Keith:** "I'll compensate."   (Page 17)
Engine revs

Cue 18   **Keith:** "Just a second."   (Page 18)
Engine revs savagely

Cue 19   **Keith:** "A mooring screw." (*3rd time*)   (Page 19)
         Hoots

Cue 20   **Mrs Hatfield:** "... it is pulling me."   (Page 19)
         Engine rev

Cue 21   **June:** "I've got it."   (Page 19)
         Hoots

Cue 22   **Emma:** "What, like this?"   (Page 19)
         Engine revs

Cue 23   **Keith:** "Just turn the key."   (Page 20)
         Engine dies

Cue 24   **June** and **Emma** go below   (Page 20)
         Distant hoots

Cue 25   Sunset   (Page 22)
         River wildlife noises

Cue 26   **Emma** and **Alistair** go ashore and unfasten the bow and stern (Page 25)
         lines
         Engine starts with a roar

Cue 27   **Keith:** "Coming aboard?"   (Page 25)
         Cut engine noise

Cue 28   **Emma:** "I'll do the ropes."   (Page 27)
         Engine starts

Cue 29   **Alistair:** "Here we go."   (Page 27)
         Engine goes into gear, then grating sound

Cue 30   **Alistair:** "I've got it."   (Page 28)
         Cut grating sound; engine slow ahead

Cue 31   **Alistair:** "... keeps to his side."   (Page 28)
         2 deep, loud, distant hoots

Cue 32   **Alistair** gives two hoots   (Page 28)
         2 short hoots in distance

Cue 33   **Emma** (*shouting*): "... out of the way."   (Page 28)
         2 short hoots, closer

Cue 34   **Emma:** "... just told him you were."   (Page 29)
         2 short hoots, very loud and close

Cue 35   **June** (*screaming*): "LOOK OUT!"   (Page 29)
         Enormous long hoot as steamer passes boat; crash and clatter
             from below; cut engine noise

Cue 36   **Emma** comes from saloon; **Alistair** restarts engine   (Page 30)
         Engine starts

Cue 37   **Alistair:** "... to be too pleased."   (Page 30)
         Grinding sound from under hull and threshing sound of protesting
             engine

Cue 38   **Alistair:** "I'll try."   (Page 30)
         Whirring sound

Cue 39	**Emma:** "Try again." *Whirring sound*	(Page 30)
Cue 40	**Emma:** ". . . come up front." *Whirring noise*	(Page 30)
Cue 41	**Emma:** "Try again now." *Whirring noise*	(Page 30)
Cue 42	**Emma:** "And again." *Whirring noise*	(Page 30)
Cue 43	**Alistair:** "Oh." (*He shrugs and switches off engine*) *Cut engine noise*	(Page 30)
Cue 44	**Alistair:** "Righto." *Engine starts*	(Page 31)
Cue 45	**Vince:** ". . . slow astern." *Engine slow astern*	(Page 31)
Cue 46	**Vince:** "Touch more." *Increase engine noise slightly*	(Page 32)
Cue 47	**Vince:** "Ease off." *Engine throttles back*	(Page 32)
Cue 48	**Alistair:** "Oh, yes." *Engine revs*	(Page 32)
Cue 49	**Vince:** ". . . Gessing Lock next stop, eh?" *Engine full ahead*	(Page 32)
Cue 50	**Vince:** ". . . risk the cookie, do we?" *Engine throttles back*	(Page 34)
Cue 51	**Vince:** "There you go." *Cut engine noise*	(Page 35)
Cue 52	**June** and **Vince** go below *Pause, then cork pops*	(Page 36)
Cue 53	**Vince** throws book overboard *Splash*	(Page 38)

ACT II

Cue 54	**Vince:** "There's your starter." *Engine roars into life then dies*	(Page 41)
Cue 55	**Vince:** "And then that." *Engine starts*	(Page 42)
Cue 56	**Vince:** "Start engines." *Engine starts*	(Page 44)
Cue 57	**Vince:** "Cut engine." *Cut engine noise*	(Page 46)
Cue 58	**Vince:** ". . . and switch on." *Engine starts*	(Page 46)

Cue 59	**Alistair:** "Oh, get stuffed." *Cut engine noise*	(Page 47)
Cue 60	**Emma:** "Start engines." *Engine starts*	(Page 48)
Cue 61	**Emma:** "Slow ahead, helm." *Engine slow ahead; increase to full ahead shortly*	(Page 48)
Cue 62	**Emma:** "Slow ahead." *Engine slow ahead*	(Page 51)
Cue 63	**Emma:** "Slow astern." *Engine slow astern*	(Page 51)
Cue 64	**Emma:** "Stop engines." *Cut engine noise*	(Page 51)
Cue 65	**Emma** and **June** go below *Pause, then general jollity noises—glasses, bottles opening etc.*	(Page 56)
Cue 66	**Alistair** sits aft on cabin roof *Music: James Last*	(Page 56)
Cue 67	**June** comes up on deck *Stop music*	(Page 58)
Cue 68	Aft hatch shuts; **Fleur** moves along boat *Nightbird sings; pause, then repeat*	(Page 66)
Cue 69	**Fleur:** "Start engines, Skipper." *Engine starts*	(Page 67)
Cue 70	**Fleur:** "Ease her out, Skipper." *Engine noise as boat is eased out*	(Page 68)
Cue 71	**Fleur:** "Slow ahead, Skipper." *Engine slow ahead*	(Page 68)
Cue 72	**Fleur:** "Full ahead, Skipper." *Engine full ahead*	(Page 69)
Cue 73	**Fleur:** "Bridge." *Train thunders above*	(Page 69)
Cue 74	**Fleur:** "Slow ahead, Skipper." *Engine slow ahead*	(Page 70)
Cue 75	**Fleur:** "Full astern, Skipper." *Engine full astern*	(Page 71)
Cue 76	**Fleur:** "Stop engines, Skipper." *Cut engine noise to ticking over*	(Page 71)
Cue 77	**Fleur:** "Slow ahead." *Engine slow ahead*	(Page 71)
Cue 78	**Fleur:** "Switch off." *Cut engine noise*	(Page 71)
Cue 79	**Vince** closes aft doors *Occasional thumps and bumps from aft cabin*	(Page 76)

Cue 80	As dawn breaks *Clap of thunder, rain effect*	(Page 76)
Cue 81	**Vince:** ". . . if you please." *Engine starts*	(Page 77)
Cue 82	**Vince:** ". . . coming for you." *Engine noise as craft is manoeuvred*	(Page 77)
Cue 83	**Vince:** ". . . that's enough, Ginger." *Cut engine noise*	(Page 78)
Cue 84	**Alistair:** "He won't——" *Sound of splintering wood*	(Page 78)
Cue 85	**Emma:** "Won't be a second, love." *Engine starts, then into gear and slow ahead*	(Page 83)
Cue 86	**Alistair:** "Full ahead." *Engine full ahead*	(Page 83)
Cue 87	Boat passes under bridge; **Emma** turns on cassette radio *Faint voice*	(Page 83)
Cue 88	**Alistair:** "Just the chap." **Emma** starts cassette *Cut voice, start music: "The Earl of Oxford's March" by William Byrd*	(Page 84)
Cue 89	**Alistair** throttles back *Engine throttles back; music ends*	(Page 84)
Cue 90	**Alistair:** "Dead slow ahead, Skipper." *Engine dead slow ahead*	(Page 84)
Cue 91	**Alistair:** "We'll be OK." *Sudden grinding crash; cut engine*	(Page 85)
Cue 92	When ready *Birdsong*	(Page 85)

MADE AND PRINTED IN GREAT BRITAIN BY
LATIMER TREND & COMPANY LTD PLYMOUTH

MADE IN ENGLAND